Business Email Writing:
99+ Essential Message Templates

Unstoppable Communication Skills at Work

JOHN LEWIS

TABLE OF CONTENTS

INTRODUCTION

What could be more critical to being heard and delivering your message effectively in today's age of over-communication?

If your professional path entails applying for jobs, you must have great résumés, letters, and face-to-face communication skills. To be considered for a promotion, your everyday communication must demonstrate dependability, judgment, and resourcefulness. Your success as a business owner, consultant, or other professional depends on proposals and presentations. And today, regardless of our goals, most of us desire to establish a strong internet presence. We desire to work well with others while advocating for our needs and views.

Of course, the cornerstone for all of this is... writing! Surprisingly, few individuals are aware of this. Most individuals think about presentations when they want to improve their communication skills. Knowing how to give a good speech may appear more appealing than writing, but it ignores the reality: even a 20-second elevator pitch must be written before it can be given. The written word is the foundation of all good websites, videos, Twitter campaigns, blogs, and most other communication platforms.

There's a simple explanation for this. Humans think in terms of language. Regardless of how important graphics are in a communication "product," whether print or digital, text is an essential support structure for planning.

And if only a few words appear in the final message, they must be exactly the proper ones.

Unlike the business sector, the academic system is focused on thinking about things rather than doing them. Writing for school is mostly intended to demonstrate your comprehension of what you have learned or to contribute to the store of human knowledge. Academia has historically rewarded deep, difficult, convoluted literature with costly words. This is evolving, albeit slowly.

Business writing, on the other hand, is always directed toward action. And, no matter what the goal, it is always best achieved by being approachable, direct, clear, concrete, and uncomplicated. What you write should be intriguing, convincing, and conversational.

Imitating nineteenth-century writing traditions in your work makes little sense, and attempting to write hollow, cliché-ridden twenty-first-century blog entries is a recipe for boredom. Even though no one wants to read such messages, they are all around us. As a result, learning to write well gives you a significant competitive edge and helps you stand out from the crowd.

Why Effective Business Email Writing Matters

Business email writing refers to the skill of composing effective and professional emails for various business purposes. It involves the use of proper etiquette, clear and concise language, and a professional tone to communicate with colleagues, clients, partners, or any other relevant parties.

Effective business email writing is crucial for several reasons. It plays a significant role in professional communication and can directly impact the success of individuals and organizations. Here are some key reasons why effective business email writing matters:

2

Professionalism: Email is a widely accepted form of professional communication in business. Well-crafted emails demonstrate professionalism and competence, helping to create a positive impression of the sender. By using appropriate language, tone, and formatting, you can convey your expertise, attention to detail, and respect for recipients.

Clear Communication: Effective email writing ensures your message is correctly understood. In a busy corporate environment, people receive numerous emails daily, and clear communication becomes essential to cut through the noise. By using concise and precise language, organizing your thoughts logically, and providing relevant details, you can enhance the clarity of your message and minimize the chances of misinterpretation.

Time Efficiency: Well-written emails save the sender and recipient time. A clear and concise email lets the recipient quickly understand the purpose and context, reducing the need for back-and-forth exchanges. This can lead to more efficient decision-making, task completion, and collaboration within the organization.

Professional Relationships: Effective email writing helps to build and maintain professional relationships. Polite and courteous language and appropriate greetings and sign-offs can foster a positive rapport with colleagues, clients, and stakeholders. Additionally, the ability to clearly convey your ideas and requests through email can contribute to effective teamwork and collaboration.

Reputation and Brand Image: Emails reflect the professionalism and credibility of individuals and organizations. Sloppy or poorly written emails can negatively affect your competence and attention to detail. On the other hand, well-crafted emails can enhance your reputation, promote your personal brand, and contribute to a positive image for your organization.

Persuasion and Influence: Effective business email writing can be persuasive. Whether you pitch a business proposal, negotiate terms, or seek buy-in from stakeholders, the ability to articulate your ideas clearly and convincingly can significantly impact the outcome. Employing persuasive language, structuring your arguments effectively, and addressing potential concerns can increase your chances of success.

Legal and Professional Considerations: Emails can have legal implications, and it is essential to be mindful of the content and tone when corresponding via email. Miscommunication, inappropriate language, or unprofessional conduct can lead to legal disputes, damaged relationships, or reputational harm. You can mitigate potential risks by adhering to professional standards and practicing discretion in your email communication.

In summary, effective business email writing matters because mastering the art of crafting effective emails can maximize your impact, productivity, and success in the business world.

Essential Elements of Professional Email Writing

Certainly! Professional email writing requires attention to detail and effective communication. Here are the essential elements to consider when writing professional emails:

Clear and Concise Subject Line: The subject line should accurately reflect the purpose of your email. It serves as the first point of contact between the sender and the recipient, providing a brief summary of the email's content. It should be specific and brief, giving the recipient an idea of what the email entails. A well-crafted subject line improves the chances of your email being opened and read promptly.

Professional Greeting: Professional email greetings are crucial as they set the tone for your communication and create a positive impression on the recipient. Begin your email with a proper salutation, addressing the recipient appropriately. If you are unsure about the recipient's name or title, use a generic greeting such as "Dear [Job Title]" or "Hello."

Polite and Courteous Tone: Maintain a professional and polite tone throughout the email. Be respectful and avoid using slang, jargon, or offensive language. Use courteous phrases like "please," "thank you," and "I appreciate your assistance" to convey your professionalism.

Clear and Organized Structure: Organize your email into paragraphs or bullet points to enhance readability. Each paragraph should focus on a specific topic or idea, and there should be a logical flow from one paragraph to the next. Use headings or bold text to highlight important points.

Introduction: Start with a brief introduction that states the purpose of your email. Clearly state who you are and provide any necessary context or background information. This helps the recipient understand the purpose and importance of your message from the beginning.

Body: The body refers to the main content or message of the email. It is the portion where you write the text that conveys your thoughts, ideas, or information to the recipient. The body of an email typically follows the subject line and any introductory greetings. In the body of your email, provide the necessary details, explanations, or requests. Be concise and to the point, focusing on the essential information. Use clear and straightforward language, avoiding unnecessary jargon or technical terms unless the recipient is familiar with them.

Proper Grammar and Spelling: Pay attention to grammar, spelling, and punctuation. Proofread your email before sending it to ensure accuracy. Poor grammar or spelling mistakes can create a negative impression and undermine your professionalism.

Polite and Clear Closing: End your email with a polite closing, such as "Thank you," "Best regards," or "Sincerely." Sign off with your name and contact information, if necessary. This provides a courteous and professional conclusion to your email.

Proper Attachments and Formatting: If you need to attach files, ensure they are appropriately named and clearly mentioned in the body of the email. Avoid sending large attachments, if possible. Format your email using a professional font and maintain a consistent layout throughout.

Proofreading and Editing: Before hitting the send button, proofread your email for any errors or inconsistencies. Check for clarity, tone, and overall effectiveness. Editing ensures that your message is clear, concise, and professional.

Remember, it's crucial to consider the context and relationship with the recipient when writing professional emails. Adapting your tone and style to suit the specific situation will enhance your communication and make a positive impression.

Benefits of Mastering Business Email Communication

Effective email communication is vital in building and maintaining successful professional relationships in today's digital world. Let's delve into the advantages that await those who invest time and effort into honing their email communication skills.

Professionalism and Credibility: Mastering business email communication allows you to project a professional image, reflecting positively on your personal brand and organization. By utilizing proper email etiquette, including appropriate language, grammar, and formatting, you can establish credibility and gain the trust of your recipients.

Clear and Concise Communication: Effective business email communication ensures your message is clear, concise, and easily understood. Well-structured emails with organized information and a logical flow help recipients grasp your intended meaning quickly, reducing the chances of misinterpretation or confusion.

Time Efficiency: By mastering email communication, you can save both your time and that of your recipients. Crafting concise emails with relevant subject lines and a clear call to action enables recipients to understand your message swiftly and respond promptly, enhancing overall productivity.

Enhanced Professional Relationships: Strong professional relationships are built on effective communication. You can nurture positive connections with clients, colleagues, and stakeholders by mastering business email communication. Prompt and articulate responses and a courteous tone contribute to fostering trust, respect, and collaboration.

Increased Productivity: Efficient email communication practices can significantly boost productivity. By employing concise and focused emails, you reduce the risk of overwhelming recipients with unnecessary information, ensuring they can quickly process and respond to your message. This efficiency promotes streamlined workflows and minimizes delays in decision-making processes.

Opportunities for Growth and Collaboration: Proficient email communication opens doors to new opportunities for growth and collaboration. When your emails demonstrate clarity, professionalism, and value, you increase the likelihood of receiving favorable responses. This can lead to partnerships, collaborations, career advancements, and potential business ventures.

Global Reach and Connectivity: Emails transcend geographical boundaries and time zones, allowing you to connect with individuals worldwide anytime. Mastering email communication enables you to effectively engage with a global audience, breaking down barriers and expanding your professional network.

Documentation and Reference: Emails serve as written communication records, providing documentation that can be referred to in the future. By mastering business email communication, you ensure your messages are well-documented and easily retrievable, facilitating information recall and accountability when needed.

Cost-Effective Communication: Email communication is highly cost-effective compared to traditional mail or phone calls. By mastering this form of communication, you can leverage its affordability to reach a wide audience and convey your message efficiently, saving both time and resources.

Adaptability and Convenience: Email communication offers flexibility and convenience, allowing recipients to respond at their own pace. Mastering the art of business email communication equips you with the ability to communicate effectively in various professional contexts, adapting your style and tone to suit different recipients and situations.

Investing time and effort into improving your email communication skills will unlock the potential for personal and professional growth, establishing yourself as a proficient communicator in the digital landscape.

How to Use This Book

To make the most of the "Business Email Writing Book: 99+ Essential Message Templates for Unstoppable Communication Skills at Work," follow these guidelines on how to use the book effectively:

Start with the Introduction: Begin by reading the introduction to get an overview of the book's content and understand the importance of effective business email writing.

Understand the Chapter Structure: Familiarize yourself with the book's organization. Note that it consists of several chapters, each covering different aspects of business email writing.

Begin from the Basics: Chapter 1 focuses on understanding business email writing. Learn about its importance, the key elements of well-written emails, common mistakes to avoid, and how to tailor emails to different audiences.

Explore Essential Components: Proceed to Chapter 2, which delves into the essential components of a business email. Gain insights into crafting subject lines, greetings, body content, closing remarks, and signatures effectively.

Dive into Email Templates: The book's core lies in Chapter 3, where you'll find a variety of email templates for different situations. Explore subchapters dedicated to specific scenarios such as introduction and networking, professional correspondence, sales and marketing, customer service, internal communication, and job application and interview emails. Select relevant templates that suit your needs or adapt them to your unique circumstances.

Learn Writing Techniques: Chapter 4 guides writing techniques for effective communication. Understand how to write clearly and concisely, maintain a professional tone, structure emails appropriately, use proper grammar and punctuation, and emphasize key points.

Refine Your Emails: Chapter 5 focuses on polishing your business emails. Learn about proofreading and editing techniques, avoiding common mistakes, enhancing clarity and readability, and improving email templates. Apply these tips to fine-tune your emails for maximum impact.

Utilize Additional Resources: Consult external references further to expand your knowledge and skills in this area. Follow the sample email templates for inspiration or adapt to your needs. These templates serve as practical examples of effective business email writing. Use the references provided to familiarize yourself with abbreviations and find answers to common queries.

Apply and Practice: Apply the knowledge and skills gained from the book by practicing writing effective business emails. Use the book as a reference whenever you need assistance. With consistent practice, you'll improve your communication skills over time.

Following these steps and engaging with the book's content can enhance your business email writing skills and help you become more proficient in communicating effectively at work.

THE BASICS OF BUSINESS EMAIL WRITING

Writing an effective business email requires both procedure and psychology. First, you must grasp how to format a business email, including a superb subject line, acceptable greeting, body copy, and closing. However, you must go beyond simply providing knowledge and some inspiration.

According to the researchers, every email is an interruption. It must be valuable because you're asking someone to read your email. Your email should have a purpose and explain it simply and concisely. According to Jeff Su in the Harvard Business Review, don't spend time or words getting to your point; instead, be explicit about why you're messaging and what you want.

Because we all receive hundreds of emails daily, you must work hard to prevent what academics call "standardized, vague, and impersonal realizations of interpersonal moves." Personalize your emails and keep them engaging, or you risk losing readers' attention.

Common Mistakes to Avoid in Business Emails

It's important to be aware of common mistakes to avoid in business emails to ensure that your communication is effective and professional. Here is an exhaustive explanation of these mistakes:

Poor Subject Lines: A vague or uninformative subject line can result in your email being ignored or sent to the spam folder. Avoid using generic subject lines like "Hello" or "Important Information." Instead, make it specific and relevant to the content of your email, providing recipients with a clear idea of what to expect.

Lack of Personalization: Failing to personalize your emails can make them feel generic and impersonal. Address recipients by their names and segment your email lists to send targeted and relevant content. Personalization helps establish a connection with your audience and increases engagement.

Overlooking Proofreading and Editing: Sending emails with typos, grammatical errors, or formatting issues reflects poorly on your professionalism and attention to detail. Always proofread and edit your emails thoroughly before sending them to ensure accuracy and clarity.

Lengthy and Dense Emails: Long paragraphs or walls of text can overwhelm recipients and discourage them from reading your entire email. Keep your emails concise and to the point, using clear and well-structured paragraphs, bullet points, or numbered lists to enhance readability and comprehension.

Lack of a Clear Call to Action (CTA): Not including a clear and compelling call to action in your email can result in a lack of desired response or engagement. Clearly state what you want recipients to do, whether clicking on a link, making a purchase, or replying to your email. Make the CTA stand out by using a button or highlighting it visually appealingly.

Ignoring Mobile Optimization: With a significant portion of emails being opened on mobile devices, ensuring that your emails are mobile-friendly is crucial. Neglecting mobile optimization can lead to formatting issues, poor readability, and a negative user experience. Test your emails across different devices and screen sizes to ensure they look and function well on mobile.

Lack of Segmentation and Targeting: Sending the same email to your entire subscriber list without considering their interests, preferences, or behaviors can result in low engagement and unsubscribes. Segment your email list based on relevant criteria and tailor your content to each segment's specific needs and interests.

Inconsistent Branding: Failing to maintain consistent email branding can lead to confusion and a lack of recognition. Ensure that your email templates, colors, fonts, and overall design align with your brand identity. Consistent branding builds trust and reinforces your brand's image.

Misleading or Deceptive Subject Lines and Content: Using misleading subject lines or deceptive content in an attempt to increase open rates or engagement is unethical and can damage your reputation. Be honest and transparent in your communication, delivering on the promises made in your subject line and providing valuable and relevant content to recipients.

Lack of Testing and Analytics: Neglecting to test your emails before sending them or not analyzing the performance and engagement metrics can prevent you from optimizing your campaigns. Conduct A/B testing on subject lines, content, layouts, or CTAs to determine what resonates best with your audience. Monitor email metrics like open rates, click-through rates, and conversions to identify areas for improvement.

By avoiding these common mistakes, you can enhance the effectiveness of your business emails, improve engagement with your audience, and achieve better results from your email marketing campaigns.

However, the basics of business email writing encompass fundamental principles and guidelines that help ensure effective and professional communication. Here is an exhaustive definition and explanation of the basics:

Creating a Concise, Actionable Message

Summarise the email in 6–8 words in the subject line. Including a subject in your email is critical, as emails without a subject may be ignored. Your subject line should be brief and concise, emphasizing the email's main content. The perfect subject tells the reader everything they need to know or informs them enough to make a decision. People receiving hundreds of emails daily may only open emails with interesting subject lines. Because the complete subject may not be displayed on a mobile device, prioritize the most crucial words in the subject. Subjects should be 6-8 words long and personalized for the recipient.

Examples of effective email subject lines

- Marketing meeting on June 7 at 3 p.m. Can you come?
- The printer failed. Can I get a replacement for $200?
- Your abcd.org package will arrive on September 8.

Bad email subject line examples

- A gathering
- The printer
- I'm on my way to you.

Keep emails brief. People are busy and don't have time to read work emails. Make your emails as brief as possible while still delivering the necessary information.[2] Your phrases should be brief and direct. Before sending your email, review it and remove any unnecessary material. In general, eliminate any information that is excessive or off-topic.

Some people aim to write and send emails with no more than five sentences. If you can accomplish this, it is an excellent rule of thumb for keeping an email succinct and to the point. This can be accomplished by answering the question, "Who am I? What am I looking for? Why am I approaching this individual? Why should they comply with my request? "What is the next step that I/they/we must take?" This is true for the normal email, not an email requiring a lot of detail or a short "thank you" to your coworker who provided you the link.

Format the email such that it can be quickly read and acted upon. Use formatting that will allow your reader to get the required information rapidly. In a long email, highlight the most important sentences or themes. Use bullet points and bold text to make the email easier to read and respond to.

Include URLs or attachments if they will speed up the reader's email processing. Never make the reader search for a URL or attachment in another email. Before sending the email, make sure the file is attached.

Determine what action you want the reader to take. Make it clear to the reader that you are seeking a decision, advice, a reference, or a purchase. Ask for what you want, need, or anticipate directly and unequivocally! It is especially vital to ask properly if you are sending to numerous persons. Also, specify the name of the person who needs to make the choice. "Elizabeth, would you like me to take path A or path B here?"

Alternatively, if your email only notifies someone of something rather than requesting a response, clearly identify the email with "FYI" in the subject or first sentence.

Maintaining Formality and a Professional Appearance

Establish a formal tone. Your email should have a professional and simple tone. Strive for a confident, polite tone. Try to avoid using emotive or casual language in your email. When possible, avoid contractions and abbreviations. Remember that longer phrases can appear more formal.

For instance, the following email is inappropriate for business:

"Thank you for the snakes. I'm sorry to announce that two people were killed. Please provide more soon. I'll talk to you later!"

A more formalized version of the above email:

"Thank you for delivering the four ball pythons to ABCD on March 2, 2015. Unfortunately, when I opened the snake package, two snakes appeared to have been injured during the delivery and were dead. I would appreciate it if you could deliver two replacement snakes as soon as possible. Please email me or call the store if you have any more queries or to arrange for a new shipment."

If it aligns with "work culture," a more casual email is okay "in-house" with coworkers you know well. However, avoid text abbreviations, write entire words, and don't write anything you wouldn't want your supervisor to read.

Double-check your email. Make every effort to ensure that your email is free of language and spelling errors and that it follows normal punctuation - no ALL CAPS, for example. Many email programs offer a spell-check feature; if yours does, use it! Poor grammar will almost surely undercut your message, so utilize a grammar checker if feasible.

If you are sending an email to a large group of people or if the email is essential, you should have someone (or multiple people) proofread it before sending it.

Best Practises for Formal Greetings and Closings

Depending on your relationship with the recipient, ceremonial openings and closings may be appropriate. The following sections offer some guidance and a variety of options.

Introduce yourself in your email. The greeting should be brief but formal. Depending on the context of the message, you may or may not opt to address a person by name. A message to another company or an unidentified individual does not require a name.

Here are some examples of greetings:

- Hello and good afternoon,
- Greetings,
- Dr. Smith and Mrs. Campbell,

Add a closure to your email. An acceptable closure is polite and indicates that the email has concluded. While the closing of an email may not contain a conventional letter closing such as "Best Wishes" or "Sincerely," it is regarded as a "best practice" to include a closing.

Some possible closures:

- I eagerly await your response and hope to hear from you soon.
- Thank you for your consideration.
- My best wishes,
- Thank you for taking the time to read this.

Sign your name. It is proper to include your name at the end of an email. Many email programs allow you to establish an automatic signature tailored to your preferences. Make certain that the formality of your response corresponds to the details of the communication. In a work email to another company or someone you have never met, you should provide your full name and title, although your first name alone may be fine in an email to a coworker you see daily.

Here are some examples of signatures:

- Dr. Jane Smith (in the most formal sense)
- Dr. Smith (in a less official tone)
- Jane Smith (in a more casual tone)
- Jane (casual)

Provide contact details beneath your signature. You may want to provide contact information such as your phone number, fax number, address, or website, depending on the details of the email. If you want to include this information in most or all of your emails, you may incorporate it into your personalized email signature.

Understanding the Purpose of Your Email

Understanding the purpose of your email is crucial for effective communication. It involves clearly identifying and articulating the primary objective or intention behind sending the email. Understanding the purpose allows you to structure your message appropriately, tailor the content to your audience, and achieve your desired outcome.

Understanding the purpose of your email refers to comprehending the specific goal or intention you aim to achieve by sending the email. It involves identifying the desired outcome, whether it's requesting information, seeking clarification, providing instructions, making a request, expressing gratitude, sharing updates, or any other objective relevant to your professional communication.

Importance

Clarity and Focus: When you understand the purpose of your email, you can focus your message and ensure that it conveys your intentions clearly. It helps you avoid ambiguity and unnecessary information, leading to more effective communication.

Audience Relevance: Understanding the purpose allows you to tailor your email to the needs and expectations of your recipients. It enables you to provide relevant information or address specific concerns, increasing the chances of a positive response.

Time Efficiency: Clearly defining the purpose can streamline your message and eliminate unnecessary back-and-forth communication. This helps save you and the recipient time, making your email more efficient.

Steps to Understand the Purpose of Your Email

Identify the Desired Outcome: Start by determining what you want to achieve with the email. Is it to inform, request, persuade, collaborate, or something else? Clearly define the specific objective you wish to accomplish.

Analyze the Context: Consider the broader context of the communication. Is the email related to a particular project, task, or issue? Understanding the context will help you frame your message appropriately.

Consider the Audience: Reflect on who will be receiving your email. What are their roles, responsibilities, and expectations? Understanding your audience will help you tailor your message to resonate with their needs and interests.

Determine the Key Points: Identify the main points or information you need to convey to achieve your objective. Prioritize the essential details and avoid unnecessary information that may distract from your purpose.

Craft a Clear Subject Line: A concise and descriptive subject line can help convey the purpose of your email upfront, making it easier for recipients to understand its relevance and urgency.

Structure your Email: Organize your email logically and coherently. Start with a clear introduction that highlights the purpose, provide necessary details in the body, and conclude with a call to action or next steps related to your objective.

Review and Revise: Review your message before sending it to ensure it aligns with the purpose. Check for clarity, relevance, and coherence, making any necessary revisions to strengthen your communication.

By understanding the purpose of your email and aligning your message accordingly, you can enhance the effectiveness of your communication, improve audience engagement, and increase the likelihood of achieving your desired outcome.

Structuring Your Emails for Maximum Impact

As a writer, you must treat all incoming messages as an essential contact. Everyone evaluates you based on how you write to them. As a professional writer, they want you to adhere to grammar and sentence structure standards regardless of the letter's content. It's especially vital when writing to a customer or an editor. In most cases, your email communications are the only way editors get a sense of who you are.

Previously, freelance writers would send questions and text messages by normal mail, then sit back and wait for a response. Email now allows for far faster responses. And, while it may take an editor a few days to respond to an inquiry, it is preferable to waiting weeks or even months. However, a few editors stubbornly adhere to the old ways. One online magazine editor insisted that contributors continue to send queries and manuscripts via normal mail.

Hence, structuring your emails for maximum impact involves organizing the content clearly and concisely to effectively communicate your message and achieve the desired outcome. Here's an exhaustive definition and explanation of how to structure your emails for maximum impact:

Use Clear and Concise Body Paragraphs: Break the body of the email into paragraphs, each focusing on a specific point or topic. Use clear and concise language to convey your message effectively. Consider using bullet points or numbered lists to present information in a structured and easily digestible format.

Provide Supporting Details: Elaborate on the main points in the body of the email, providing relevant details, examples, or evidence to support your statements. Use proper formatting to highlight key information, such as bold or italicized text.

Utilize White Space and Paragraph Breaks: Make your email visually appealing and easy to read by incorporating white space between paragraphs and using paragraph breaks when transitioning to a new topic. This enhances readability and comprehension.

Use Headings and Subheadings: If your email contains multiple sections or topics, consider using headings or subheadings to provide a clear structure and guide the recipient's attention. Headings help break down the email's content and allow the recipient to quickly navigate to specific sections.

Include Clear Call-to-Action: Clearly state what action or response you expect from the recipient. Use a direct and specific call-to-action to avoid confusion and ensure that the recipient understands what is required of them.

Conclude with a Polite Closing: End the email with a courteous closing, such as "Best regards" or "Sincerely," followed by your name and contact information. This provides a professional and polite conclusion to the email.

Proofread and Edit: Before sending the email, thoroughly proofread and edit it for clarity, grammar, and spelling errors. Ensure that the email is error-free and conveys your message accurately.

Consider Email Length: While providing necessary information is important, be mindful of the email length. Long, overwhelming emails may deter the recipient from reading or comprehending the content. Aim for concise and focused communication.

Consider the Recipient's Perspective: Put yourself in the recipient's shoes and consider how they would perceive and understand your email. Anticipate potential questions or concerns they may have and address them proactively to provide a comprehensive and informative email.

By following these guidelines and structuring your emails in a logical and organized manner, you can maximize the impact of your communication, increase clarity, and improve the likelihood of achieving your desired outcomes.

Using Proper Salutations and Sign-offs

Using Proper Salutations and Sign-offs in business email writing is crucial for maintaining a professional and respectful tone. Let's define and explain each aspect in detail:

Salutations

Salutations are greetings used at the beginning of an email to address the recipient. They serve as an opening courtesy and help establish a polite and professional tone. Here are some key points to consider:

Formal Salutations: When writing to someone you don't have a close relationship with or when communicating in a professional setting, it's important to use formal salutations. Examples include "Dear Mr. Smith," "Dear Ms. Johnson," or "Dear Dr. Patel." Use the recipient's appropriate title (Mr., Ms., Dr., etc.) followed by their last name.

Informal Salutations: Informal salutations are suitable for more casual or familiar relationships in a professional context. If you have an established rapport with the recipient, you can use salutations like "Hello John," "Hi Sarah," or "Dear Alex," using their first name.

Unknown Recipient: If you're unsure about the recipient's name or if you're sending a mass email, you can use a more general salutation like "Dear Team," "Dear Hiring Manager," or "To Whom It May Concern."

Sign-offs

Sign-offs, also known as valedictions or closing remarks, are phrases used to conclude an email politely. They signify respect and provide closure to your message. Here are some commonly used sign-offs:

Formal Sign-offs: Using sign-offs that reflect professionalism and respect in formal or professional settings is best. Examples include "Sincerely," "Kind regards," "Best regards," or "Yours faithfully." These phrases convey a sense of formality and professionalism.

Informal Sign-offs: If you have a more familiar or casual relationship with the recipient, you can use sign-offs that reflect that tone. Examples include "Best," "Warm regards," "Thanks," or "Take care." These phrases are less formal but still maintain a polite and friendly tone.

Tailoring Sign-offs: Consider the context and purpose of your email when choosing a sign-off. For example, if you're requesting a favor, you may choose a slightly more persuasive sign-off like "Looking forward to your response," or if you're expressing gratitude, you can use "Thank you again for your assistance."

Signature: Include a signature block below your closing remark in addition to the sign-off. This typically includes your full name, job title, company name, contact information (phone number, email address), and any other relevant details that provide professional identification.

Remember to always tailor your salutations and sign-offs to the recipient and the formality required in your email's context. Pay attention to cultural and organizational norms as well. Using proper salutations and sign-offs demonstrates professionalism, respect, and proper email etiquette, enhancing effective communication in a business setting.

Tailoring Your Emails to Different Audiences

Businesses must be able to tailor their emails to different audiences. It assists you in communicating the value of your product, convincing new customers, and establishing trust and loyalty. But how can you build and deliver messages that appeal to multiple buyer demographics, platforms, and stages? Here are some pointers to help you create successful and compelling messaging for your intended audience.

Recognize Your Target Demographics

Before you begin writing or developing your communications, you must first determine who you are communicating with. What are their concerns, aims, requirements, and preferences? What factors influence their decisions, how they absorb information, and how they interact with your product? Surveys, interviews, personas, user testing, and analytics can all be used to investigate and categorize your audiences. The more you understand about your target audiences, the better you will be able to personalize your messaging to their specific context and expectations.

Establish Your Value Proposition

Your value proposition is the central statement that describes how your product solves a problem, provides a benefit, or satisfies a desire of your target audience. It should be simple, succinct, and persuasive and address Why people should select your product over others? To create a compelling value proposition, you must first understand your product's features, benefits, distinctions, and your target audience's difficulties, motivations, and objections. To help you articulate your value proposition, you might use frameworks such as the value proposition canvas or the unique selling proposition.

Change Your Tone and Style

Your tone and style are the words, images, and sounds you use to convey your messages. They reflect your brand's personality, voice, and values and affect how your audiences perceive and respond to your communications. To tailor your tone and style to diverse audiences, consider their demographics, psychographics, culture, and emotions. For example, for a B2B audience, you may use a more professional and authoritative tone, whereas, for a B2C audience, you would use a more casual and welcoming tone. You can also employ different colors, fonts, symbols, and media types to meet your audience's preferences and attention spans.

Match Your Messages to the Buyer's Path.

The buyer journey is the path your prospects take from being aware of their problem to contemplating your solution, making a purchase, and becoming committed advocates. Your audiences have distinct questions, worries, and ambitions at each stage of the buyer journey, and they require different sorts of information and help. To connect your communications with the buyer journey, map out the steps, touchpoints, and information your consumers will encounter along the process, and then customize your messages to their individual requirements and interests. For example, you could use more informative and awareness-raising messages at the top of the funnel, while at the bottom, you could use more persuading and action-oriented messages.

Test and Improve Your Emails

Adapting your messages to different audiences is a continuous process of learning and growth. You must evaluate and measure the effectiveness of your messages and then optimize them based on feedback and statistics. A/B testing, heatmaps, click-through rates, conversion rates, and user feedback are all tools and strategies for testing and optimizing your messages. You may reach your product marketing goals by testing and tweaking your communications to ensure they are relevant, engaging, and impactful for your audiences.

Personalization is Key

Personalization is crucial for your intended audience to see and understand your message. According to Statista, marketing customization is extremely or somewhat appealing to 90% of US customers. According to SmarterHQ studies, 72% of customers claim they only engage with personalized messaging.

Take into account the customer's journey and objective. Ascertain that the email you're attempting to convey resonates with their wants and gives value through entertainment, offers, or solutions to their problem areas.

Examine the facts you've gathered about your consumers to personalize an email for diverse audiences effectively. This information allows you to construct buyer personas, segment audiences, and produce personalized content. However, the tailored experience should not end there; ensure that your website exposes different clients to distinct information, offers, and messaging to appeal to them directly.

EMAIL TEMPLATES FOR DIFFERENT SITUATIONS

In the fast-paced and competitive world of business, effective communication is paramount. Among the most common forms of professional correspondence, business emails are central to fostering productive relationships, driving sales, and conveying critical information. Crafting compelling and well-structured emails can be time-consuming, especially when faced with various scenarios that require tailored messages. This is where email templates for different situations prove to be invaluable tools for professionals seeking to streamline their communication process and enhance their email writing prowess.

Email templates are pre-designed formats that offer a framework for composing emails in specific situations. These templates serve as a foundation for building personalized and relevant messages, saving time and effort while ensuring consistency and professionalism. As a business email expert, understanding the diverse scenarios that warrant different communication approaches is key to harnessing the full potential of email templates.

This guide will explore various email templates for various business scenarios. Whether you need to reach out to a potential client, follow up on a sales inquiry, respond to customer feedback, or request an informational interview, our collection of email templates covers it all. These templates have been carefully crafted to address each situation's nuances and specific needs, enabling you to adapt and customize them to suit your unique requirements.

As we delve into each scenario, we will provide you with ready-to-use templates and offer valuable insights into the elements that make these emails effective. We will discuss the art of personalization, the significance of a compelling subject line, the importance of addressing the recipient appropriately, and the use of a professional tone that aligns with each circumstance.

As we explore the various email templates for different situations, you will gain a deeper understanding of the subtleties that make each type of communication unique. Whether you are seeking to build strong business relationships, close deals, provide exceptional customer service, or make a compelling case for your job application, our email templates will empower you to communicate with precision and confidence.

Whether you are a seasoned professional or just starting your career, these templates will equip you with the tools and knowledge to excel in your communication skills, ultimately leading to stronger connections, increased productivity, and remarkable success in your professional journey. So, let's embark on this transformative journey together and unlock the true potential of your business email communication.

Introduction and Networking Emails

Introduction and networking emails are crucial to building professional relationships, expanding your network, and exploring new opportunities. These emails serve as initial points of contact, enabling you to introduce yourself, establish rapport, and create meaningful connections with individuals in your industry or field of interest. Effective introductions and networking emails require careful attention to detail, a professional tone, and a clear purpose. This section provides a range of email templates specifically designed to help you navigate these initial interactions successfully.

Introduction emails allow you to make a positive first impression and showcase your professional background, skills, or areas of expertise. These emails are often used when reaching out to potential clients, industry experts, colleagues, or individuals you admire. A well-crafted introduction email can pique their interest, demonstrate your value, and establish a foundation for further collaboration or discussion.

On the other hand, networking emails serve as a tool to build and strengthen connections within your industry. These emails may involve requesting informational interviews, seeking advice, or simply expressing interest in someone's work. By leveraging networking emails effectively, you can foster relationships, gain insights, and open doors to new opportunities.

Within this section, you'll find a collection of introduction and networking email templates for various scenarios. Whether seeking professional guidance, expanding your network, or initiating collaborations, these templates provide a framework to communicate your intentions and effectively make a positive impression.

While these email templates offer a solid starting point, it's important to personalize them according to your specific circumstances and the recipient's interests. Tailoring each email ensures that your message resonates and reflects your genuine enthusiasm for connecting and building mutually beneficial relationships.

By utilizing these introduction and networking email templates, you'll be equipped with the tools to confidently reach out to individuals in your industry, establish meaningful connections, and seize valuable opportunities for professional growth and collaboration. Remember, building a strong network starts with a well-crafted introduction, and nurturing those connections can lead to a wealth of possibilities in your career or business endeavors.

Templates

V1. Reaching out to a Potential Client (#001)

Introduction and Potential Collaboration

Dear [Client's Name],

I hope this email finds you well. My name is [Your Name], and I am reaching out to introduce myself and explore potential collaboration opportunities. I recently came across your work at [mention specific event, publication, or project], and I was impressed by the innovative approach and impact you have made in [relevant industry/field].

As a [your professional background], I specialize in [specific expertise or skills]. I believe that our shared interests and complementary strengths could potentially lead to a fruitful partnership. I would love to discuss how we can mutually benefit each other and achieve common goals.

If you're open to it, I would appreciate the opportunity to set up a call or meeting at your convenience. I am eager to learn more about your vision and explore potential areas of collaboration.

Thank you for considering my request. I look forward to the possibility of working together.

Warm regards,

[Your Name]

[Your Contact Information]

V2. Requesting an Informational Interview (#002)

Request for Informational Interview

Dear [Contact's Name],

I hope this email finds you well. My name is [Your Name], and I am a [your professional background or current role] with a keen interest in [industry/field of interest]. I recently came across your work and achievements in [specific area or project], and your expertise and accomplishments have inspired me.

I would greatly appreciate the opportunity to learn from your experience and gain insights into your career journey. I am particularly interested in understanding [specific topic or aspect of their work]. Your expertise and perspective would be invaluable in guiding me as I navigate my own professional path.

I would be honored to speak with you if you would be available for a brief informational interview, whether in person or over a phone call. I am flexible regarding the time and location and more than happy to accommodate your schedule.

Thank you for considering my request. I greatly appreciate your time and expertise. I look forward to the possibility of connecting and learning from you.

Best regards,

[Your Name]

[Your Contact Information]

V3. Connecting with Industry Professionals (#003)

Connecting and Sharing Insights

Dear [Recipient's Name],

I hope this email finds you well. My name is [Your Name], and I am contacting professionals in the [industry/field] and exchanging insights and ideas.

I have been following your work and contributions to [industry/field] for some time and have found your expertise and perspectives inspiring. I am particularly drawn to your expertise in [specific area or project], which aligns closely with my own professional interests.

I would love to connect with you virtually or in-person to share thoughts on [industry trends/topics] and explore potential synergies. Your unique insights and experiences would provide valuable guidance as I continue to grow in my career.

Please let me know if you would be open to a brief conversation or meeting at a convenient time. I am excited about the possibility of connecting with you and exchanging ideas.

Thank you for your time and consideration. I look forward to hearing from you.

Sincerely,

[Your Name]

[Your Contact Information]

V4. Requesting a Recommendation (#004)

Request for Recommendation

Dear [Contact's Name],

I hope this email finds you well. I have been following your work closely and have been truly impressed by your expertise and achievements in [industry/field]. I admire your unique perspective and value the insights you bring to the table.

I am writing to request a recommendation from you kindly. As I pursue [specific goal, opportunity, or career transition], I believe your endorsement would greatly enhance my profile and credibility. Your firsthand knowledge of my skills and qualifications would carry significant weight, and I would be honored to have your support.

If you are willing to provide a recommendation, I would be happy to provide any necessary information or further details to assist you in writing it. Please let me know your preferred method of communication and any specific information you may need from me.

Thank you for considering my request. I genuinely appreciate your time and support and am grateful for the opportunity to work alongside professionals like yourself.

Warm regards,

[Your Name]

[Your Contact Information]

V5. Connecting with Industry Peer (#005)

Introduction and Shared Interests

Dear [Recipient's Name],

I hope this email finds you well. I wanted to reach out and introduce myself as a fellow professional in the [industry/field]. I have been following your work and accomplishments and find your expertise and contributions inspiring.

As someone passionate about [specific area or topic], I believe that we share common interests and goals. I would love to connect and exchange insights, ideas, and experiences. Collaborating with like-minded professionals like yourself fosters growth and innovation within our industry.

If you're open to it, I would be delighted to connect over a call, meet in person to explore areas of potential collaboration further, or simply engage in a meaningful conversation about our shared interests.

Thank you for considering my invitation. I look forward to the possibility of connecting with and learning from each other.

Best regards,

[Your Name]

[Your Contact Information]

Professional Correspondence

Professional correspondence is a formal communication between individuals or organizations in a business or professional context. It encompasses a wide range of written communication, including emails, letters, memos, and other forms of written correspondence.

Effective professional correspondence is essential for maintaining professional relationships, conveying information accurately, and achieving specific objectives. Whether you're communicating with clients, colleagues, partners, or other professionals, it's crucial to uphold a high standard of professionalism and adhere to established communication norms.

Types of Professional Correspondence

Business Letters: Formal letters are often used for official communication, such as formal invitations, business proposals, complaint letters, or cover letters for job applications. Business letters follow specific formats and conventions, including proper salutations, subject lines, body content, and closing remarks.

Email Communication: Emails are the most common form of professional correspondence in today's digital age. They are used for various purposes, including requesting information, providing updates, scheduling meetings, sending reports, and following up on discussions. Professional emails should be concise, well-structured, and convey a professional tone.

Memos: Memos, or memorandums, are internal written communications used within organizations. They are typically used to convey important information, announce policy changes, share updates, or provide instructions. Memos should be clear, concise, and organized, with a professional tone appropriate for the workplace.

Reports: Reports are comprehensive documents that present information, analysis, and findings on a particular topic or project. They are often used to communicate research results, financial data, project updates, or performance evaluations. Reports should be well-structured, objective and present information logically and professionally.

Professional correspondence is crucial in establishing and maintaining professional relationships, conveying information effectively, and achieving business objectives. However, we will focus on business letters and talk about other aspects later.

Templates

V1. Request for Information or Assistance (#006)

Request for [Specific Information/Assistance]

Dear [Recipient's Name],

I hope this email finds you well. I am kindly requesting your assistance with [specific information/issue]. I believe your expertise in [relevant area] would be invaluable in addressing this matter.

[Provide background or context for the request]. If possible, I would greatly appreciate your prompt response.

Thank you in advance for your time and support.

Best regards,

[Your Name]

V2. Meeting Request (#007)

Request for Meeting: [Topic/Purpose]

Dear [Recipient's Name],

I hope this email finds you well. I would like to request a meeting with you to discuss [specific topic or purpose]. Your insights and expertise in this area would be highly valuable.

I am available [provide specific date(s) and time(s)] or am open to suggestions based on your availability. Please let me know a convenient time for you, and I will adjust my schedule accordingly.

Thank you for considering my request. I look forward to meeting with you.

Kind regards,

[Your Name]

V3. Follow-up on Previous Conversation (#008)

Following Up on [Topic/Discussion]

Dear [Recipient's Name],

I hope you're doing well. I wanted to follow up on our recent conversation regarding [specific topic/discussion]. I found our discussion [insightful/valuable], and I would like to revisit some key points.

[Summarize the key points or decisions made during the previous conversation]. I would appreciate being informed if there have been any updates or progress since our last conversation.

Thank you for your attention to this matter. I look forward to hearing from you.

Best regards,

[Your Name]

V4. Acknowledgment and Confirmation (#009)

Confirmation of [Specific Matter]

Dear [Recipient's Name],

I would like to confirm [specific matter] as discussed [mention the date or occasion of the discussion]. It was a pleasure speaking with you, and I appreciate the opportunity to clarify and confirm the details.

[Summarize the confirmed details or arrangements]. If any additional documents or information are required, please let me know, and I will provide them promptly.

Thank you for your attention to this matter. If you have any further questions or concerns, please don't hesitate to reach out.

Warm regards,

[Your Name]

V5. Expressing Gratitude (#010)

Appreciation for [Specific Action/Support]

Dear [Recipient's Name],

I wanted to take a moment to express my heartfelt gratitude for your [specific action/support]. Your assistance in [describe the impact or benefit] has been invaluable and greatly appreciated.

[Provide additional details or express how the recipient's action has positively affected you or the project]. Individuals like you make a significant difference, and I am sincerely grateful for your dedication.

Once again, thank you for your [kindness/support/assistance]. It means a lot to me.

Best regards,

[Your Name]

Customer Service Emails

In the realm of customer service, effective communication plays a pivotal role in building and maintaining strong relationships with customers. Customer service emails are vital to this communication, allowing businesses to address inquiries, resolve issues, and provide exceptional customer support.

Customer service emails are a direct line of communication between customers and businesses. They offer a written record of interactions, enabling both parties to refer back to the details of conversations, ensuring clarity and accountability. Whether it's responding to inquiries, handling complaints, or providing post-purchase assistance, well-crafted customer service emails are essential for delivering exceptional customer experiences.

Writing customer service emails involves empathizing with customers, understanding their concerns, and providing relevant and timely solutions. Effective customer service emails should be clear, concise, and customer-focused. They should demonstrate a genuine desire to assist customers, regardless of the nature or complexity of the issue.

Customer service emails cover many scenarios, including product inquiries, order updates, returns and exchanges, troubleshooting, and more. Each scenario requires a tailored approach to address the customer's specific needs and concerns effectively. While there may not be a one-size-fits-all solution, having a strong foundation of customer service email templates can significantly enhance the efficiency and effectiveness of your communication.

The primary goal of customer service emails is to provide customers with timely, accurate, and helpful information. They should promptly address customer inquiries, offer appropriate solutions, and ensure customers feel valued and supported. Additionally, customer service emails should maintain a professional and friendly tone, fostering a positive impression of the business and reinforcing trust and loyalty.

In today's digitally interconnected world, customer service emails are often the first line of contact for customers seeking assistance. As a result, they significantly impact customer satisfaction, brand reputation, and overall customer experience. By mastering the art of crafting exceptional customer service emails, businesses can elevate their customer service efforts and foster long-lasting relationships with their customers.

In this collection of customer service email templates, you'll find a range of scenarios and situations commonly encountered in customer service interactions. These templates serve as a starting point, providing structure and guidance for effectively addressing customer needs. However, it's essential to tailor and personalize each email to the specific context and customer to ensure a more personalized and meaningful interaction.

| Templates

V1. *Responding to a Customer Inquiry* (#011)

Your Inquiry about [Product/Service]

Dear [Customer's Name],

Thank you for reaching out to us with your inquiry regarding [product/service]. We appreciate your interest in our offerings.

[Provide a detailed response to the customer's inquiry, addressing all their questions or concerns].

If you have any further queries, please don't hesitate to reach out to us. We are here to assist you.

Best regards,

[Your Name]

[Your Position]

[Company Name]

[Contact Information]

V2. *Resolving a Customer Complaint* (#012)

Resolution for [Customer Complaint]

Dear [Customer's Name],

We sincerely apologize for the inconvenience caused by the issue you experienced with [product/service]. We understand the frustration this may have caused and appreciate you bringing it to our attention.

[Acknowledge the specific complaint and describe the steps taken to resolve the issue].

As a gesture of goodwill, we would like to offer [compensation/offering] to ensure your satisfaction.

We value your feedback, as it helps us improve our products and services. Please let us know if you have any further concerns or require additional assistance.

Thank you for your understanding and patience.

Kind regards,

[Your Name]

[Your Position]

[Company Name]

[Contact Information]

V3. Handling a Return or Exchange Request (#013)

Return/Exchange Request for [Product/Order]

Dear [Customer's Name],

Thank you for contacting us regarding your return/exchange request for [product/order]. We apologize for any inconvenience caused and will assist you with the process.

[Provide instructions on the return/exchange process, including any relevant requirements or procedures].

Once we receive the returned item or process the exchange, we will [mention the next steps or timeframe].

If you have any further questions or need clarification, please feel free to reach out to us.

Best regards,

[Your Name]

[Your Position]

[Company Name]

[Contact Information]

V4: Requesting Customer Feedback (#014)

We Value Your Feedback

Dear [Customer's Name],

At [Company Name], we strive to provide exceptional products and services. Your feedback is crucial in helping us improve and meet your expectations. We kindly request a few minutes of your time to share your thoughts and experiences with us.

[Provide a brief explanation of the feedback process, such as a survey, review, or direct contact method].

We greatly appreciate your participation and value your opinion. Thank you for being a valued customer.

Best regards,

[Your Name]

[Your Position]

[Company Name]

[Contact Information]

V5: Addressing Late Delivery (#015)

Update on Late Delivery for [Order/Package]

Dear [Customer's Name],

We apologize for the delay in delivering your [order/package]. We understand the frustration this may have caused and sincerely apologize for any inconvenience.

[Provide a brief explanation for the delay, such as logistical issues or unforeseen circumstances].

Rest assured, we are actively working to resolve this issue and expedite delivery. We expect your [order/package] to arrive by [new estimated delivery date].

If you have any further concerns or require additional assistance, please don't hesitate to reach out to us.

Thank you for your understanding and patience.

Kind regards,

[Your Name]

[Your Position]

[Company Name]

[Contact Information]

V6: Responding to Positive Feedback/Testimonial (#016)

Thank You for Your Positive Feedback

Dear [Customer's Name],

Thank you for sharing your positive feedback and kind words regarding our [product/service]. We greatly appreciate your support and are thrilled to hear about your positive experience.

[Express your gratitude and mention specific aspects of the feedback/testimonial that stood out].

Your satisfaction is our top priority, and we will continue to work hard to provide excellent products and services.

If you have any further feedback or need any assistance, please feel free to contact us. We value your continued support.

Best regards,

[Your Name]

[Your Position]

[Company Name]

[Contact Information]

V7: Responding to Negative Feedback/Testimonial (#017)

Acknowledging Your Feedback

Dear [Customer's Name],

Thank you for sharing your feedback regarding our [product/service]. We sincerely apologize for any dissatisfaction caused and appreciate you bringing this matter to our attention.

[Express your understanding of the customer's concerns and commitment to addressing the issue].

We value your feedback and would like to assure you that we take this matter seriously. Our team is actively investigating and working on a resolution.

We appreciate your patience and understanding during this process. If you have any further questions or require additional information, please don't hesitate to reach out to us.

Best regards,

[Your Name]

[Your Position]

[Company Name]

[Contact Information]

V8: *Requesting Customer Testimonials/Reviews* (#018)

Share Your Experience with [Company Name]

Dear [Customer's Name],

We hope you are enjoying your [product/service] from [Company Name]. We would be thrilled if you could take a moment to share your experience and leave a testimonial or review.

[Explain the importance of customer testimonials/reviews and how they help other customers make informed decisions].

We greatly appreciate your time and support. Thank you for being a valued customer.

Best regards,

[Your Name]

[Your Position]

[Company Name]

[Contact Information]

V9: *Informing Customers about Product Updates or Upgrades* (#019)

Exciting Product Update for [Product/Service]

Dear [Customer's Name],

We are delighted to inform you about an exciting update or upgrade to our [product/service]. We believe this enhancement will further improve your experience and satisfaction.

[Provide a brief overview of the update or upgrade and how it benefits the customer].

If you have any questions or need further assistance, please feel free to contact our support team. We value your continued support.

Thank you for choosing [Company Name].

Warm regards,

[Your Name]

[Your Position]

[Company Name]

[Contact Information]

V10: Apologizing for Billing or Payment Error (#020)

Apology for Billing/Payment Error

Dear [Customer's Name],

We would like to sincerely apologize for the billing/payment error related to your recent [invoice/statement]. We understand the inconvenience and frustration this may have caused.

[Explain the nature of the error, the steps taken to rectify it, and any additional information or assistance provided].

Rest assured. We have addressed the issue and taken measures to ensure it does not occur again in the future. If you have any further questions or concerns, please don't hesitate to reach out to us.

Thank you for your understanding and patience.

Best regards,

[Your Name]

[Your Position]

[Company Name]

[Contact Information]

Internal Communication

Internal communication refers to the exchange of information, ideas, and messages within an organization among its employees, teams, and departments. It is vital to running a successful and efficient business, as effective internal communication fosters collaboration, enhances productivity, boosts employee engagement, and helps align everyone toward common goals. Internal communication can take place through various channels, including:

Email: The most common and widely used form of internal communication for sending official announcements, updates, and sharing information.

Intranet: A secure internal network that hosts company-related resources, documents, and updates accessible only to employees.

Instant Messaging: Real-time chat platforms for quick discussions, team collaboration, and information sharing.

Internal Social Media: Company-specific social media platforms that encourage sharing, discussions, and networking among employees.

Meetings: Face-to-face or virtual gatherings where employees exchange ideas, discuss projects and receive updates from management.

Newsletters and Memos: Regularly distributed publications that provide employees with updates, achievements, and important information.

Types of Internal Communication

Top-Down Communication: Information flows from management or higher-ups to employees, often used for announcements, directives, and company-wide updates.

Bottom-Up Communication: Information flows from employees to management, providing feedback, suggestions, and concerns from the front lines.

Horizontal or Lateral Communication: Information exchanged among colleagues at the same level, promoting collaboration and sharing of ideas within departments or teams.

Diagonal Communication: Information is shared across different levels and departments to ensure better coordination and problem-solving.

Benefits of Effective Internal Communication

Employee Engagement: Employees who are well-informed feel more engaged and connected to the company's mission and values.

Team Collaboration: Efficient communication fosters collaboration, improving teamwork and project outcomes.

Company Culture: Transparent communication helps build a positive company culture where employees feel valued and included.

Alignment: Clear communication ensures everyone is on the same page and working towards common objectives.

Productivity: Reduced misunderstandings and improved information flow lead to higher productivity levels.

Employee Satisfaction: Effective internal communication contributes to employee satisfaction and retention.

To improve internal communication, organizations should invest in creating a culture of openness and transparency, providing various channels for communication, encouraging feedback, and addressing challenges proactively. Internal communication becomes a powerful tool for fostering a thriving and cohesive workplace when done right.

Templates

V1. Team Meeting Announcement (#021)

Upcoming Team Meeting: [Date/Time]

Dear [Team/Department],

I hope this email finds you well. I am writing to announce our next team meeting, scheduled for [date] at [time]. The meeting will take place in [location or virtual platform].

Agenda:

- [Agenda item 1]
- [Agenda item 2]

- [Agenda item 3]
- [Agenda item 4]

Please come prepared to discuss these topics, and if you have any additional items to include in the agenda, let me know before [date]. Your active participation is vital, and I look forward to seeing you all there.

Best regards,

[Your Name]

[Your Title/Department]

[Contact Information]

V2. Policy Update Notification (#022)

Important: [Policy Name] Update

Dear all

I hope this email finds you well. We wanted to inform you about a recent update to our [Policy Name]. The changes will be effective from [date], and each team member must familiarize themselves with the revised policy.

You can find the updated policy attached to this email or access it through [location or link]. If you have any questions or need further clarification, please don't hesitate to reach out to [Contact Name].

Thank you for your attention to this matter.

Best regards,

[Your Name]

[Your Title/Department]

[Contact Information]

***V3**. Employee Appreciation* (#023)

Recognizing [Employee Name]'s Contributions

Dear [Team/Department],

I am delighted to take a moment to recognize and appreciate [Employee Name] 's outstanding contributions to our team. Their dedication, hard work, and positive attitude have significantly impacted [project or team success].

Please join me in expressing our gratitude and congratulating [Employee Name] for their exceptional efforts.

Best regards,

[Your Name]

[Your Title/Department]

[Contact Information]

***V4**. Task Assignment and Deadline* (#024)

Task Assignment: [Task Description]

Dear [Team Member],

I hope this email finds you well. I am assigning you the task of [Task Description], which needs to be completed by [Deadline Date]. Please find the relevant details and resources attached to this email.

If you have any questions or need assistance with the task, please feel free to approach me or [Supervisor/Colleague Name].

Thank you for your commitment to excellence.

Best regards,

[Your Name]

[Your Title/Department]

[Contact Information]

V5. Project Update (#025)

Project [Project Name] Status Update

Dear all

I would like to provide you with an update on the status of [Project Name]. As of [date], we have accomplished the following milestones:

- [Milestone 1]
- [Milestone 2]
- [Milestone 3]

We are currently on track to meet the project deadline. However, we are facing some challenges in [specific area] and actively working on resolving them.

If you have any questions or suggestions, please don't hesitate to share them.

Thank you for your continued support.

Best regards,

[Your Name]

[Your Title/Department]

[Contact Information]

V6. Employee Training Invitation (#026)

Employee Training Session: [Topic]

Dear [Team/Department],

We are pleased to invite you to a training session on [Topic]. The training will take place on [date] at [time] in [location or virtual platform].

The training aims to enhance our skills in [specific area] and is facilitated by [Trainer Name], a seasoned expert in the field.

Please confirm your attendance by [RSVP date], so we can make the necessary arrangements.

Looking forward to seeing you there.

Best regards,

[Your Name]

[Your Title/Department]

[Contact Information]

Job Application and Interview Emails

These types of emails play a pivotal role in the job application process and are vital for job seekers and employers alike. Here are some key reasons why these emails are so significant:

First Impressions: Job Application and Interview Emails are often the first point of contact between a candidate and a potential employer. They create the initial impression of the candidate's professionalism, communication skills, and attention to detail. A well-crafted email can set a positive tone from the outset, increasing the chances of the candidate being considered for the position.

Personalization: These emails allow candidates to tailor their applications and showcase their enthusiasm for the specific job and company. Customizing the email demonstrates genuine interest and dedication, making the candidate stand out among other applicants.

Professionalism: Job Application and Interview Emails reflect a candidate's professionalism and ability to adhere to business etiquette. Properly formatted and error-free emails show that the candidate takes the application seriously and respects the employer's time.

Clear Communication: Effective communication is crucial in the hiring process. These emails allow candidates to express their qualifications, relevant experiences, and motivations concisely and persuasively. On the employer's side, it facilitates conveying important details about the interview process and the next steps.

Following Instructions: Employers often include specific instructions in job postings for how to apply. Candidates who follow these instructions and submit a well-structured application email demonstrate their ability to pay attention to details and follow directions.

Brand Representation: For employers, Interview Emails present an opportunity to represent their brand and company culture. Employers can leave a positive impression on potential hires by crafting a thoughtful and welcoming interview invitation.

Interview Confirmation: Interview Emails confirm the scheduled interview for both candidates and employers. This reduces the chances of miscommunication and ensures that both parties are on the same page regarding the interview's date, time, and location.

Establishing Rapport: Well-written Interview Emails create an atmosphere of professionalism and warmth. Candidates feel respected and valued, while employers can establish rapport with potential employees before meeting them in person.

Documentation: Job Application and Interview Emails are essential documentation during the hiring process. Employers can refer back to emails when making decisions, and candidates can use them to track their application progress and interview schedules.

Templates

V1. Job Application Email Template (#027)

Application for [Job Title] Position

Dear [Hiring Manager's Name],

I hope this email finds you well. I am writing to express my strong interest in the [Job Title] position at [Company Name], as advertised on [Job Board/Company Website]. I believe my skills and experience align perfectly with the requirements outlined in the job description.

[Share a brief introduction about yourself, highlighting relevant qualifications and accomplishments.]

I have attached my resume for your review, which provides further details on my professional background. I am excited about the opportunity to contribute my expertise to the success of [Company Name] and would be thrilled to discuss how my skills can benefit your team.

Thank you for considering my application. I look forward to the possibility of speaking with you further.

Sincerely,

[Your Name]

[Your Contact Information]

V2. Interview Confirmation Email Template (#028)

Interview Confirmation - [Job Title] Position

Dear [Interviewer's Name],

I hope this email finds you well. I am writing to confirm my availability for the interview scheduled for [Date] at [Time] for the [Job Title] position at [Company Name].

I am looking forward to discussing my qualifications and experiences in more detail and learning more about the opportunities at [Company Name]. Please let me know if there are any specific documents or references I should bring to the interview.

Should there be any changes in the interview schedule, kindly let me know, and I will do my best to accommodate the new time.

Thank you for considering my application. I am excited to meet with you and the [Company Name] team.

Best regards,

[Your Name]

[Your Contact Information]

V3. Follow-up Email After Interview Template (#029)

Thank You for the Interview - [Job Title] Position

Dear [Interviewer's Name],

I hope this email finds you well. I am sincerely grateful for the opportunity to interview for the [Job Title] position at [Company Name].

It was a pleasure discussing my qualifications and experiences with you. After learning more about [Company Name] 's vision and culture during the interview, I am even more enthusiastic about the prospect of joining your team.

I am confident that my skills and passion align perfectly with the [Job Title] role, and I am eager to contribute my expertise to the success of [Company Name].

Please feel free to reach out if you require additional information or have further questions.

Thank you once again for your time and consideration.

Best regards,

[Your Name]

[Your Contact Information]

V4. Second Follow-up Email Template (Post-Interview) (#030)

Checking on Interview Status - [Job Title] Position

Dear [Interviewer's Name],

I hope this email finds you well. I wanted to follow up on the interview we had for the [Job Title] position at [Company Name] on [Date].

I am still very interested in joining [Company Name] and contributing my skills to the team. I understand that the selection process may take some time, and I wanted to reiterate my enthusiasm for the position.

If there are any updates on the status of my application or any additional information you need from me, please do not hesitate to let me know.

Once again, thank you for your time and consideration.

Best regards,

[Your Name]

[Your Contact Information]

V5. Rejection Response Email Template (#031)

Thank You for Considering My Application - [Job Title] Position

Dear [Hiring Manager's Name],

I hope this email finds you well. I wanted to thank you for considering my application for the [Job Title] position at [Company Name].

While I am disappointed to hear that I was not selected for the role, I truly appreciate the opportunity to be considered as a candidate. I am confident that the experience of applying and interviewing at [Company Name] has been valuable for my professional growth.

I would be delighted to stay connected and learn about future opportunities at [Company Name].

Thank you once again for your time and consideration.

Best regards,
[Your Name]
[Your Contact Information]

V6. Acceptance of Job Offer Email Template (#032)

Acceptance of Job Offer - [Job Title] Position

Dear [Hiring Manager's Name],

I hope this email finds you well. I am thrilled to formally accept the offer for the [Job Title] position at [Company Name].

I am excited about the opportunity to join the [Company Name] team and contribute my skills to the growth and success of the organization. I am grateful for your trust in me and look forward to starting on [Start Date].

Please let me know if there are any specific onboarding or paperwork requirements I should be aware of before my start date.

Once again, thank you for the offer, and I am excited to begin this new chapter with [Company Name].

Best regards,
[Your Name]
[Your Contact Information]

COMMON EMAIL TEMPLATES FOR EVERYDAY COMMUNICATION

Effective communication is the backbone of successful professional relationships in the fast-paced world of modern business. Among the various communication channels, email continues to be the primary means of exchanging information, ideas, and updates in workplaces across the globe. However, crafting well-written, concise, clear, and engaging emails can be time-consuming, especially when facing a barrage of messages daily. This is where common email templates for everyday communication come to the rescue.

Common email templates are pre-designed formats offering ready-to-use frameworks for different communication scenarios. They serve as invaluable tools for busy professionals, providing them with a streamlined approach to crafting emails for recurring situations. Whether it's sending a quick thank-you note, responding to an inquiry, scheduling a meeting, or conveying important updates, these templates save time, ensure consistency, and enhance communication skills.

This chapter on common email templates for everyday communication will explore various pre-written formats catering to diverse business needs.

Why Use Common Email Templates?

Efficiency: Time is a valuable resource in any professional setting. With common email templates, professionals can swiftly address routine communication needs without reinventing the wheel each time. Templates allow for quick customization, so you can fine-tune the message's content to suit the specific context.

Consistency: Consistency in communication is vital for brand identity and professional reputation. Using standardized email templates ensures that your business maintains a unified voice and image across all interactions, fostering trust and credibility among recipients.

Clarity and Conciseness: Effective communication demands clarity and conciseness. Common email templates are designed to present information logically, with emphasis on the most important details. This approach enhances understanding and reduces the risk of miscommunication.

Professionalism: Maintaining a professional image is essential as a business email expert. Common email templates are thoughtfully crafted to reflect professionalism, which is crucial when dealing with clients, superiors, and other stakeholders.

Adaptability: While templates provide a structured framework, they are versatile enough to adapt to specific situations. Customization options ensure that you can add a personal touch or address individual concerns while benefiting from pre-prepared content's convenience.

Incorporating these common email templates into your everyday communication can elevate your business email writing skills, save valuable time, and establish a professional and consistent communication approach that sets you apart in today's competitive business landscape. Let's dive in and explore the power of common email templates for everyday communication!

Requesting Information or Clarification

Requesting information or clarification in emails is essential for effective communication and ensuring that all parties involved understand the topic. This role plays a crucial part in various aspects of business communication:

Gathering Essential Data: When you need specific data, facts, or figures to make informed decisions or complete a task, requesting information through email is an efficient way to collect the necessary details. This could include market research data, financial reports, customer feedback, or any other relevant information.

Seeking Clarification: Sometimes, business emails may contain complex or ambiguous content. In such cases, requesting clarification helps avoid misunderstandings and ensures that everyone involved is on the same page. By seeking clarification, you demonstrate your commitment to understanding the matter thoroughly.

Resolving Issues: If a situation arises where the information provided is unclear, incomplete, or contradictory, requesting further details or clarification can be a proactive step toward resolving the issue. Promptly seeking the right information can prevent misunderstandings and potential conflicts.

Confirming Instructions or Requests: In business email exchanges, it's common to receive instructions or requests from colleagues, clients, or superiors. When you want to confirm your understanding of these instructions or requests, responding with a clarifying email ensures that you are on track and meeting expectations.

Improving Collaboration: Requesting information or clarification fosters open communication and transparency among team members. By encouraging a culture of seeking and providing clear information, you create an environment conducive to collaboration and effective teamwork.

Strengthening Relationships: When you ask for information or clarification courteously and respectfully, it demonstrates your interest in the other person's perspective and input. This can foster stronger professional relationships built on trust and mutual understanding.

Demonstrating Professionalism: Proactively seeking necessary information or clarifying doubts showcases your professionalism. It shows you are attentive to details, committed to accuracy, and invested in producing high-quality work.

When drafting an email requesting information or clarification, ensure your message is clear, concise, and polite. Clearly state what information you need or what aspect requires clarification. Be specific and avoid vague language to reduce the risk of misunderstandings.

Templates

V1. Requesting Information on a Project Status (#033)

Request for Project Status Update

Dear [Recipient's Name],

I hope this email finds you well. I wanted to inquire about the current status of [Project Name]. As [mention the deadline or milestone] is approaching, I'd appreciate an update on the progress and any potential challenges faced by the team.

Specifically, I'd like to know:

1. What stage is the project currently in?
2. Are there any pending tasks or deliverables?
3. Have there been any deviations from the original project plan, and if so, how are they being addressed?
4. Are there any resource constraints affecting the project's progress?

Please provide this information at your earliest convenience. Please let me know if there's anything I can do to support the team or if additional resources are required.

Thank you for your attention to this matter.

Best regards,

[Your Name]

[Your Title/Position]

[Your Contact Information]

V2. Seeking Clarification on a Proposal (#034)

Clarification Request for [Project/Proposal Name]

Dear [Recipient's Name],

I hope this email finds you well. Thank you for sharing the [Project/Proposal Name] with us. After reviewing the proposal, I have a few questions to seek clarification on some points:

1. Regarding [specific point in the proposal], could you please provide more details or examples to illustrate how this will be implemented?

2. I noticed that [mention any potential discrepancies or unclear aspects]. Can you provide further explanation to address these concerns?

3. What are the projected timelines for each phase of the project, and are there any critical milestones we should be aware of?

Your insights and answers to these questions will help us better understand the proposal and evaluate its alignment with our requirements.

I look forward to receiving your response soon. Thank you for your cooperation.

Sincerely,

[Your Name]

[Your Title/Position]

[Your Contact Information]

V3. Requesting Information on a Product or Service (#035)

Inquiry About [Product/Service Name]

Dear [Recipient's Name],

I hope this email finds you well. I am reaching out to inquire about the [Product/Service Name] offered by your company. I am particularly interested in understanding the following:

1. What are the key features and functionalities of the [Product/Service Name]?

2. Can you provide pricing information or any available discounts for bulk purchases?

3. Are there any customer testimonials or case studies showcasing the effectiveness of your [Product/Service Name]?

If possible, I would appreciate receiving a product brochure or additional materials that can help me make an informed decision.

Thank you for your time and consideration. I am looking forward to your prompt response.

Best regards,

[Your Name]

[Your Title/Position]

[Your Contact Information]

V4. Requesting Clarification on a Document (#036)

Clarification Needed on [Document/Project Name]

Dear [Recipient's Name],

I hope you're doing well. I recently received [mention the document or project name], and I have a few points that require clarification to move forward with the task effectively. Specifically, I would appreciate further details on the following:

1. [Clarification Point 1]
2. [Clarification Point 2]
3. [Clarification Point 3]

Your prompt attention to this matter would be highly appreciated. Please don't hesitate to ask if you need any further information from me.

Thank you for your cooperation.

Best regards,

[Your Name]

[Your Position/Title]

[Your Contact Information]

V5. Requesting Clarity on Meeting Details (#037)

Clarification Needed for Upcoming Meeting

Dear [Recipient's Name],

I hope this email finds you well. We have an upcoming meeting scheduled for [date and time], and I would like to clarify a few details to ensure its success. Can you please provide the following information:

1. [Clarification Request 1]
2. [Clarification Request 2]
3. [Clarification Request 3]

Your assistance in providing these details will be greatly appreciated. If there are any changes or updates, please let me know as soon as possible.

Thank you, and looking forward to the meeting.

Best regards,

[Your Name]

[Your Position/Title]

[Your Contact Information]

V6: Requesting Clarity on a Policy or Procedure (#038)

Request for Clarification on [Policy/Procedure Name]

Dear [Recipient's Name],

I hope you are doing well. I am writing to seek clarity on the recently implemented [policy/procedure name]. I have a few questions that I believe need addressing to ensure compliance and understanding among our team members. Kindly provide information on the following points:

1. [Clarification Point 1]
2. [Clarification Point 2]
3. [Clarification Point 3]

Your timely response would be valuable in helping us adapt smoothly to the new policy. Thank you for your cooperation.

Sincerely,

[Your Name]

[Your Position/Title]

[Your Contact Information]

Providing Updates or Progress Reports

Providing updates or progress reports is vital to effective organizational communication. The role of these emails is to inform relevant stakeholders about the status of ongoing projects, tasks, or initiatives. They serve several essential purposes:

Transparency: Updates and progress reports promote transparency within the organization. Employees, managers, and stakeholders can stay informed about developments, challenges, and achievements by sharing information on the status of various projects or tasks.

Accountability: Regular updates create a sense of accountability among team members. When everyone knows their progress is being monitored and reported, they are more likely to stay focused and motivated to achieve their goals.

Decision-Making: Management often relies on timely and accurate information to make informed decisions. Progress reports provide the necessary data to assess the effectiveness of current strategies, identify potential roadblocks, and determine necessary adjustments or resource allocation.

Alignment: Updates help in keeping everyone aligned with the organization's objectives. By sharing progress and achievements, employees can see how their individual efforts contribute to the company's overall success, fostering a sense of purpose and teamwork.

Client or Stakeholder Communication: In some cases, progress reports are shared with clients or external stakeholders to keep them updated on the status of a project or service. Transparent communication builds trust and confidence in the organization's ability to deliver on promises.

Proactive Problem Solving: Progress reports often highlight any challenges or obstacles encountered during the project. This early identification of issues allows teams to address problems proactively, minimizing potential risks and delays.

Documentation: Progress reports serve as a record of project milestones and accomplishments over time. They provide a historical reference for future analysis, audits, or evaluations.

By embracing the role of providing updates or progress reports, businesses can enhance communication, foster collaboration, and ultimately improve the efficiency and success of their projects and operations.

Templates

V1. Weekly Progress Report (#039)

Weekly Progress Report - [Project/Task Name]

Dear [Recipient's Name],

I hope this email finds you well. As promised, here's the weekly progress report for [Project/Task Name]:

1. Accomplishments this week:
   - [Briefly list key tasks or milestones achieved]

2. Ongoing activities:
   - [Briefly mention tasks currently in progress]

3. Roadblocks/Challenges:
   - [Identify any issues or obstacles hindering progress]

4. Next steps:
   - [Outline the plan for the upcoming week]

Please let me know if you require any additional information or have any questions. I'm available to discuss any concerns or updates further.

Thank you for your attention to this report.

Best regards,

[Your Name]

[Your Title/Position]

[Your Contact Information]

V2. Quarterly Departmental Update (#040)

Quarterly Departmental Update - [Department Name]

Dear [Recipient's Name],

I hope this email finds you in good spirits. I'm pleased to share the quarterly update for [Department Name]:

1. Departmental Highlights:
   - [Summarize significant achievements and successes]

2. Team Performance:
   - [Highlight key performance indicators and metrics]

3. Ongoing Projects:
   - [Provide a status update on current departmental projects]

4. Staffing and Resource Updates:
   - [Briefly mention any changes in staffing or resource allocation]

5. Challenges and Strategies:
   - [Address any challenges and the strategies being implemented]

Your feedback and insights are highly valued. If you have any questions or suggestions, please don't hesitate to share them with us.

Thank you for your attention.

Best regards,

[Your Name]

[Your Title/Position]

[Your Contact Information]

V3. Sales Progress Report (#041)

Sales Progress Report - [Time Period]

Dear [Recipient's Name],

I trust you're having a productive day. As part of our commitment to transparency, here's a concise sales progress report for [Time Period]:

1. Total Sales Revenue:
    - [Provide the total revenue generated during the specified period]

2. Sales Targets Achieved:
    - [Highlight sales targets met or exceeded]

3. Sales Pipeline:
    - [Briefly discuss the status of potential deals in the pipeline]

4. Sales Activities:
    - [Mention key sales activities undertaken during this period]

5. Sales Forecast:
    - [Offer an outlook for the upcoming sales period]

If you require further details or want to discuss any aspect of our sales performance, please feel free to contact me.

Thank you for your attention.

Best regards,

[Your Name]

[Your Title/Position]

[Your Contact Information]

V4. Project Milestone Completion Report (#042)

Project Milestone Completion Report - [Milestone Name]

Dear [Recipient's Name],

I hope this email finds you well. I'm pleased to announce the successful completion of [Milestone Name] in [Project Name]:

1. Milestone Description:
    - [Briefly describe the milestone achieved]

2. Achievements:
    - [Summarize the objectives met and deliverables achieved]

3. Team Acknowledgment:
    - [Recognize the efforts and contributions of the team]

4. Next Milestone and Timeline:
    - [Outline the upcoming milestone and its expected completion date]

Please let me know if you need additional information or have questions regarding this milestone or the project's progress.

Thank you for your continued support.

Sincerely,

[Your Name]

[Your Title/Position]

[Your Contact Information]

Confirming Attendance or Declining Invitations

Confirming your attendance or declining invitations promptly and politely demonstrates professionalism. It shows that you value the sender's time and effort in inviting you and that you take business commitments seriously. It's also a sign of respect. It allows the organizer to plan accordingly, knowing the number of attendees, and make necessary adjustments to the event or meeting. Other reasons include:

Efficient Event Planning: By confirming your attendance, you help event organizers make logistical arrangements, such as booking venues, preparing materials, and arranging catering, with greater accuracy. Declining invitations early help prevent unnecessary expenses and wasted resources.

Building Positive Relationships: Responding to invitations, even if declining, in a courteous manner fosters positive relationships with colleagues, clients, and business partners. It shows that you value their invitations and are appreciative of their consideration.

Avoiding Miscommunication: Confirming your attendance eliminates any ambiguity about your participation, preventing misunderstandings that could arise from assumptions or lack of communication.

Demonstrating Reliability: Consistently confirming your attendance and honoring your commitments portrays you as a reliable professional. This trustworthiness can be crucial for building strong business relationships.

Flexibility and Courtesy: If you are declining an invitation, offering alternative options, such as suggesting an alternative time for a meeting or expressing interest in future events, showcase your flexibility and courtesy.

Time Management: Responding to invitations promptly allows you to manage your schedule more efficiently. It helps you avoid double bookings and ensures you can allocate appropriate time to attend essential events or meetings.

Remember, prompt and courteous communication regarding attendance or declination reflects positively on your professional image and contributes to effective business etiquette.

Templates

V1. Confirming Attendance (#043)

[Event/Meeting Name] - Confirming My Attendance

Dear [Organizer's Name],

I hope this email finds you well. Thank you for inviting me to [Event/Meeting Name] on [Date] at [Time]. I am delighted to confirm my attendance and look forward to being part of the event.

Please be assured that I will be there on time and fully prepared to actively participate in the discussions and contribute to the event's success.

If any specific materials or preparations are required from attendees, kindly let me know, and I'll ensure everything is in order beforehand.

Once again, thank you for the invitation. I appreciate the opportunity and am excited to engage with everyone at [Event/Meeting Name].

Best regards,

[Your Name]

[Your Title/Position]

[Your Contact Information]

V2. Regretful Decline (#044)

Regretful Decline for [Event/Meeting Name] on [Date]

Dear [Organizer's Name],

I hope this email finds you well. I sincerely appreciate your kind invitation to [Event/Meeting Name] on [Date] at [Time]. However, I regret to inform you that I cannot attend due to unforeseen commitments.

I apologize for any inconvenience my absence may cause and assure you that I would have loved to be part of the event. If there is any way I can still contribute or support the event remotely, please let me know, and I'll be more than willing to assist.

Once again, thank you for thinking of me and including me in the invitation list. I hope the [Event/Meeting Name] is a resounding success.

Wishing you all the best for the event.

Sincerely,

[Your Name]

[Your Title/Position]

[Your Contact Information]

V3. Polite Decline with Alternative (#045)

Declining Invitation to [Event/Meeting Name] - Offering an Alternative

Dear [Organizer's Name],

I hope this email finds you well. Thank you for inviting me to [Event/Meeting Name] on [Date] at [Time]. I genuinely appreciate the gesture and the opportunity to be part of such an important event.

However, I regret to inform you that I have a prior commitment that coincides with the event, and I won't be able to attend as planned. I apologize for any inconvenience this may cause.

To make up for my absence, I would be more than happy to offer an alternative. If you would like, I can provide a brief video message or a presentation to be played during the event to share my insights or contributions. Please let me know if this option works for you and how I can assist you further.

Once again, thank you for considering me for [Event/Meeting Name]. I hope the event is a great success, and I look forward to opportunities to collaborate in the future.

Best regards,

[Your Name]

[Your Title/Position]

[Your Contact Information]

Acknowledging Receipt of Documents or Payments

When you receive important documents or payments from clients, customers, or business partners, promptly acknowledging them helps establish trust, provides assurance, and ensures a smooth workflow. Here's why it's essential:

Confirming Transaction Completion: Acknowledging the receipt of documents or payments serves as a confirmation that the transaction has been completed successfully. It reassures the sender that their submission or payment has reached the intended recipient and is being processed.

Professionalism and Courtesy: Sending an acknowledgment email demonstrates professionalism and courtesy in your business interactions. It shows that you value the sender's efforts and time, which helps build a positive relationship.

Avoiding Misunderstandings: An acknowledgment email helps prevent misunderstandings and miscommunications. By confirming the receipt of specific documents or payments, both parties are on the same page about what has been sent and received.

Meeting Expectations: Acknowledging receipt promptly aligns with common business practices. It shows that your organization is efficient and reliable, meeting the sender's expectations for a timely response.

Addressing Inquiries: Sometimes, senders may have questions or concerns about the submitted documents or payments. By acknowledging receipt, you provide an opportunity for them to follow up if needed, ensuring any potential issues are addressed promptly.

Tracking and Record-Keeping: Acknowledgment emails create a transaction record, which can be valuable for both parties. It helps with tracking the timeline of communications and provides a reference in case of any future queries or disputes.

Compliance and Legal Purposes: In certain industries or for specific types of documents or payments, acknowledging receipt may be a legal or regulatory requirement. Ensuring compliance with such obligations is crucial to avoid any legal consequences.

Templates

V1. Acknowledgment of Receipt of Documents (#046)

Acknowledgment of Document Receipt

Dear [Sender's Name],

I hope this email finds you well. I am writing to confirm the receipt of the documents you sent on [date]. We have successfully received the following items:

1. [Document Name 1]
2. [Document Name 2]
3. [Document Name 3]

Thank you for promptly providing us with the necessary documents. Our team will review them thoroughly, and if any further action is required, we will reach out to you accordingly.

Should you have any questions or require additional information, please do not hesitate to contact me directly.

Once again, we appreciate your cooperation and look forward to working together on this matter.

Best regards,

[Your Name]

[Your Title]

[Your Company]

[Email Address]

[Phone Number]

V2. Acknowledgment of Receipt of Payment (#047)

Payment Received - Thank You!

Dear [Customer's Name],

Thank you for your recent payment of [Amount] received on [Date]. We acknowledge the successful receipt of your payment for Invoice #[Invoice Number] related to [Product/Service].

The payment has been processed and applied to your account. If you have any questions about your payment or need further assistance, please feel free to reach out to our accounts department at [Email Address] or [Phone Number].

We value your continued support and prompt attention to this matter. Please contact us if you require any information about your account status or other concerns.

Once again, we sincerely appreciate your timely payment and look forward to serving you in the future.

Best regards,

[Your Name]

[Your Title]

[Your Company]

[Email Address]

[Phone Number]

V3. Acknowledgment of Receipt of Important Documents (#048)

Receipt of Confidential Documents

Dear [Sender's Name],

I hope this email finds you well. I am writing to acknowledge the receipt of the important and confidential documents you sent to us on [Date].

We understand the sensitivity and significance of these documents, and I assure you that they will be treated with the utmost confidentiality and handled in accordance with our company's security protocols.

Our team will begin reviewing the materials, and if any further actions are required, we will be sure to inform you promptly.

If you have any concerns or require any updates regarding the processing of these documents, please feel free to contact me directly.

Thank you for trusting us with this important matter. We appreciate your cooperation and look forward to further assisting you.

Best regards,

[Your Name]

[Your Title]

[Your Company]

[Email Address]

[Phone Number]

Expressing Appreciation or Gratitude

Expressing appreciation or gratitude is vital in building and maintaining positive professional relationships. It involves acknowledging and thanking individuals for their contributions, assistance, support, or positive impact on your work or business. Here are some key reasons why expressing appreciation is important in business emails:

Strengthening Relationships: Expressing gratitude in business emails helps strengthen the bond between colleagues, clients, partners, and other stakeholders. It shows that you value and acknowledge their efforts, fostering trust and mutual respect.

Motivating and Encouraging: Expressing appreciation for someone's hard work or achievements serves as positive reinforcement. This can motivate individuals to continue performing at their best and boosts their morale and job satisfaction.

Cultivating a Positive Work Culture: A culture of gratitude and appreciation can contribute to a positive and supportive work environment. Employees feel more valued and recognized, leading to higher job satisfaction and improved teamwork.

Building Brand Loyalty: Expressing gratitude to customers or clients for their business creates a sense of loyalty. They are more likely to return for repeat purchases and recommend your products or services to others.

Handling Customer Service: Expressing appreciation in customer service emails can defuse tense situations and turn unhappy customers into satisfied ones. Showing empathy and thanking them for their feedback can go a long way in resolving issues amicably.

Networking and Relationship Building: When networking or building new business relationships, expressing gratitude after a meeting or event reinforces your interest in connecting further and leaves a positive impression.

Enhancing Professionalism: Gratitude in business emails adds a touch of professionalism and courtesy to your communication. It reflects well on your character and demonstrates that you value and acknowledge the contributions of others.

Tips for Expressing Appreciation in Business Emails

- **Be Specific**: Mention the specific actions or support for which you are expressing gratitude. Avoid generic statements and focus on the individual's unique contributions.

- **Be Genuine**: Sincerity is essential when expressing appreciation. Make sure your gratitude comes across as heartfelt and authentic.

- **Timeliness**: Send your appreciation emails promptly after the event or action that deserves acknowledgment. It shows that you value their efforts enough to respond promptly.

- **Personalize the Message**: Tailor your appreciation emails to the individual or group you are addressing. Use their names and include personalized details to make the message more meaningful.

- **Brief and Clear**: Keep your appreciation emails concise and to the point. Avoid unnecessary details or unrelated information.

- **Use Positive Language**: Employ positive and uplifting language in your email. Focus on the positive impact rather than dwelling on negative aspects.

- **Follow-Up**: If appropriate, consider following up on the recipient's response to your appreciation email or sending a periodic thank-you note to maintain the relationship.

By expressing appreciation or gratitude in your business emails, you can foster a positive and supportive professional environment, strengthen relationships, and leave a lasting impression on colleagues, clients, and business partners.

Templates

V1. Thank-You for your Support or Assistance (#049)

Gratitude for Your Support

Dear [Recipient's Name],

I hope this email finds you well. I wanted to take a moment to express my sincere gratitude for the exceptional support and assistance you provided during [mention the specific project or situation]. Your dedication and expertise were instrumental in achieving our goals, and I genuinely appreciate your effort.

Your willingness to go above and beyond has not gone unnoticed, and your commitment to excellence inspires me. It's a pleasure working with someone as talented and reliable as you.

Once again, thank you for your valuable contributions. Your hard work and collaboration have made a significant difference, and I look forward to more successful ventures together.

Best regards,

[Your Name]

[Your Title/Department]

[Your Company]

V2. Thank-You for a Successful Event or Meeting (#050)

Appreciation for a Successful [Event/Meeting]

Dear [Recipient's Name],

I hope you are doing well. I wanted to extend my heartfelt appreciation for your significant role in making [mention the event/meeting name] a great success.

Your dedication to planning, organizing, and executing the event/meeting was outstanding. Your attention to detail and ability to handle any challenges that arose truly impressed everyone involved. It was evident that you put in tremendous effort to ensure everything ran smoothly.

The positive feedback we received from participants and attendees is a testament to your hard work and commitment to excellence. We couldn't have achieved such fantastic results without you.

Once again, thank you for your exceptional contribution. Your professionalism and expertise make you an invaluable asset to our team.

With gratitude,

[Your Name]

[Your Title/Department]

[Your Company]

V3. *Gratitude for a Job Well Done (#051)*

A Heartfelt Thank-You for Your Outstanding Work

Dear [Recipient's Name],

I trust you are doing well. I wanted to take a moment to express my most profound appreciation for the outstanding job you did on [mention the project/task]. Your dedication, creativity, and attention to detail were evident throughout the entire process.

Your contributions have exceeded our expectations, and the results speak for themselves. Your hard work and commitment to excellence have significantly impacted our team's success.

Working with someone of your caliber is a privilege, and I want to extend my gratitude for consistently delivering exceptional work.

Thank you again for your valuable efforts. Your professionalism and passion for what you do set a fantastic example for all of us.

Warmest regards,

[Your Name]

[Your Title/Department]

[Your Company]

ADVANCED EMAIL TEMPLATES FOR SPECIFIC SITUATIONS

As previously mentioned, mail remains a pivotal tool for professionals to connect, collaborate, and convey ideas among the various communication channels. However, crafting the perfect business email for specific situations can be daunting, often requiring a delicate balance of clarity, persuasion, and professionalism.

While generic email templates are useful for standard communication, advanced email templates tailored to specific situations can elevate your communication skills to new heights. These templates are meticulously designed to cater to the unique requirements of various professional scenarios, ensuring that your messages resonate with precision and finesse.

This chapter delves into the world of advanced email templates for specific situations. Whether you're reaching out to potential clients, handling customer inquiries, conducting internal communications, or seeking new career opportunities, this resource will equip you with a diverse collection of email templates that are strategically crafted to yield exceptional outcomes. Our expertly curated templates cover an array of situations that business professionals commonly encounter, from networking and job applications to sales and customer service interactions.

In this digital age where communication is often rushed, mastering the art of crafting exceptional business emails can set you apart from the competition and establish your reputation as a polished and influential professional. The insights and skills gained from this guide will empower you to confidently navigate complex communication scenarios, ensuring that your messages cut through the noise and resonate with recipients, ultimately driving success in your business endeavors.

Get ready to unlock the full potential of your communication skills through our meticulously curated collection of advanced email templates for specific situations. Whether you are a seasoned professional seeking to refine your approach or a newcomer aiming to make a strong impression, this guide is your ultimate resource for mastering the art of impactful business email writing. Let's embark on this journey together and elevate your communication prowess to new heights.

Dealing with Difficult or Challenging Colleagues

Dealing with challenging colleagues requires a delicate approach to maintaining professionalism and fostering a positive working environment. While emails may not solve all interpersonal issues, they can effectively address concerns and set boundaries. Here are some strategies for handling such situations through email communication:

Choose the Right Time and Medium: Consider the urgency and sensitivity of the matter before sending an email. For less critical issues, email may be appropriate, but for more serious concerns, a face-to-face conversation might be more suitable. Email can be useful for documenting the discussion and providing a record of the communication.

Maintain a Calm and Professional Tone: When drafting the email, keep your tone neutral, respectful, and professional. Avoid using aggressive or confrontational language, as it may escalate the situation. Focus on the facts and the specific behavior or issue you want to address.

Be Specific and Objective: Clearly outline the problematic behavior or issue you're facing, providing specific examples if possible. Avoid making personal attacks or generalizations. Stick to the facts and objective observations.

Express Your Concerns: Communicate how the challenging behavior or situation is affecting you and your work. Use "I" statements to express your feelings rather than placing blame on the colleague. For example, "I feel stressed when..." or "I have difficulty completing my tasks because..."

Propose Solutions: Offer potential solutions or suggestions for addressing the issue. Be constructive and open to finding a resolution together. For instance, "Perhaps we can set up a regular meeting to discuss our project's progress" or "Let's work on improving communication by using shared task management software."

Seek Clarification: If you're uncertain about the colleague's intentions or actions, use the email to seek clarification. Ask questions in a non-confrontational manner to gain a better understanding of their perspective.

Set Boundaries: Clearly define your boundaries and expectations if necessary. Be assertive in a professional way and communicate your willingness to collaborate when everyone respects those boundaries.

Avoid CC or BCC Unless Necessary: Unless it's vital for others to be aware of the situation, avoid copying colleagues (CC) or using blind carbon copy (BCC). This could escalate the situation or make your colleague feel attacked.

Be Open to Dialogue: Encourage open communication and express your willingness to discuss the matter further. Provide your colleague with an opportunity to share their perspective and concerns.

Follow-Up: After sending the email, allow your colleague some time to process the information. If they respond positively, continue the discussion. If they don't reply or the issue persists, consider arranging a face-to-face meeting to address the matter further.

Email communication should be used as a starting point to address challenging situations, but it's essential to be open to face-to-face conversations or other forms of communication if necessary. The ultimate goal is to find constructive solutions and maintain a harmonious work environment.

Templates

V1. Setting Boundaries (#052)

Clarifying Boundaries and Expectations

Dear [Colleague's Name],

I hope this email finds you well. I wanted to take a moment to discuss some concerns that have arisen recently regarding our working relationship. While I value our collaboration, I believe clarifying some boundaries and expectations would benefit us to ensure a more productive and harmonious working environment.

Moving forward, let's agree on the following points:

1. Communicate directly about any issues or conflicts that arise.
2. Respect each other's time and schedule, ensuring timely responses to urgent matters.
3. Provide constructive feedback professionally and courteously.

I believe that open communication and mutual respect are essential to our success as a team. If you have any additional suggestions or concerns, I am more than willing to discuss them further.

Thank you for your understanding and cooperation.

Best regards,

[Your Name]

V2. Addressing Unprofessional Behavior (#053)

Professional Conduct in the Workplace

Dear [Colleague's Name],

I hope you are doing well. I am writing to address a recent incident that caused some discomfort within the team. It is essential that we maintain a professional and respectful environment at work to ensure everyone's well-being and productivity.

I kindly request that we avoid using inappropriate language, making derogatory comments, or engaging in unprofessional behavior. Let's foster an atmosphere of respect and support where each team member feels valued and appreciated.

Please don't hesitate to reach out if you have any concerns or would like to discuss this matter further.

Thank you for your cooperation.

Sincerely,

[Your Name]

V3. Requesting Improvement in Collaboration (#054)

Strengthening Our Collaboration

Dear [Colleague's Name],

I hope this email finds you well. I have noticed some challenges in our collaboration lately, and I believe we must address them to achieve better results.

Let's work on:

1. Improving communication and sharing relevant information promptly.
2. Listening actively to each other's perspectives and ideas.
3. Resolving conflicts constructively and professionally.

Focusing on these aspects can enhance teamwork and create a more positive work environment. Please let me know if you have any suggestions or if there's anything I can do to support our collaboration further.

Thank you.

Best regards,

[Your Name]

V4. Dealing with Excessive Interruptions (#055)

Respectful Communication During Work Hours

Dear [Colleague's Name],

I hope this email finds you well. I wanted to discuss an issue that has been affecting my workflow lately. I've noticed increased interruptions during work hours, which can be challenging to manage effectively.

To maintain productivity, I kindly request that we try to minimize non-urgent interruptions during focused work periods. Perhaps we could schedule specific times for discussions or address urgent matters via email or instant messaging.

I appreciate your understanding and am sure finding a balance will benefit both of us.

Thank you for your cooperation.

Sincerely,

[Your Name]

V5. *Handling Constant Negativity (#056)*

Encouraging a Positive Work Environment

Dear [Colleague's Name],

I hope all is well. I wanted to address a recurring pattern of negativity I noticed during team interactions. Maintaining a positive and encouraging work environment is crucial for our team's success and well-being.

Let's make an effort to focus on solutions rather than dwelling on problems. Constructive feedback is essential, but let's frame it positively and be supportive. Promoting a more optimistic atmosphere can boost team morale and foster greater collaboration.

If there are specific concerns you'd like to discuss, I'm here to listen and work together on finding solutions.

Thank you for your cooperation.

Best regards,

[Your Name]

Resolving Conflicts or Misunderstandings

Resolving conflicts or misunderstandings through email requires finesse, empathy, and clear communication. Here are some essential steps and strategies to effectively handle such situations:

Address the Issue Promptly: When you become aware of a conflict or misunderstanding, don't delay addressing it. Sending an email promptly can prevent the situation from escalating and show that you take the matter seriously.

Clarify the Misunderstanding: Begin by acknowledging a misunderstanding. Politely state that you've noticed some confusion or disagreement and that you'd like to address it to ensure effective communication.

Seek Common Ground: Look for points of agreement or shared goals between you and the other party. Emphasize areas where you both align and acknowledge any positive aspects of the relationship or situation.

Use "I" Statements: When discussing your perspective, use "I" statements to express your feelings and thoughts without assigning blame. For example, say, "I felt confused when..." or "I believe there may have been a miscommunication about..."

Listen Actively: If the other party has expressed their concerns or perspective, carefully read and consider their email. By paraphrasing or summarizing their key messages, you'll show that you've understood their points.

Provide Clear Explanations: Clarify your position, ensuring your points are easily understood. Use bullet points or numbered lists to break down complex issues and make your email more digestible.

Offer Solutions: Propose potential solutions or compromises to resolve the conflict. Be open to discussion and negotiation to find a mutually beneficial outcome. Conclude your email with a positive and forward-looking tone. Express your willingness to work collaboratively to resolve the conflict and reinforce the value of maintaining a constructive relationship.

Follow-Up: If the issue is not immediately resolved, offer to discuss it further via a call or in-person meeting. Some conflicts may require more extensive dialogue to find a resolution. Also, try to keep the resolution process confined to the involved parties unless absolutely necessary. Involving others may complicate matters and potentially escalate the conflict.

Stay focused on finding a resolution, and be willing to adapt your approach as needed. Communicating with clarity, respect, and understanding can foster a positive atmosphere for conflict resolution in a business context.

Templates

V1. Acknowledging the Conflict (#057)

Acknowledgment of Concern

Dear [Recipient's Name],

I hope this email finds you well. I wanted to address an issue that has come to my attention and express my sincere commitment to resolving it amicably.

I understand there might be a misunderstanding or conflict regarding [specify the nature of the conflict]. Please know that I take this matter seriously and want to ensure that we can find a resolution that satisfies all parties involved.

I would appreciate the opportunity to discuss this matter in person or over a call to understand your perspective better. Let's work together to find a mutually agreeable solution and strengthen our working relationship moving forward.

Please let me know your availability for a meeting or call, and we can schedule a time that works for both of us.

Thank you for your understanding and cooperation.

Best regards,

[Your Name]

[Your Title/Position]

[Your Contact Information]

V2. Clarifying Misunderstandings (#058)

Clarification and Resolution

Dear [Recipient's Name],

I hope this email reaches you in good spirits. It has come to my attention that there might be a misunderstanding regarding [specify the issue]. I would like to take this opportunity to clarify any misconceptions and find a way forward together.

After reviewing the situation, I believe the miscommunication stemmed from [explain the possible cause of the misunderstanding]. To ensure we are on the same page, I propose that we [offer a possible solution or compromise].

I value our working relationship and want to address this matter promptly. If you have any further concerns or suggestions, please feel free to share them, as open communication is key to resolving any issue.

Let's arrange a meeting to discuss this matter further at your earliest convenience. I am committed to finding a resolution that benefits all parties involved.

Thank you for your cooperation and understanding.

Sincerely,

[Your Name]

[Your Title/Position]

[Your Contact Information]

V3. Apologizing and Seeking Reconciliation(#059)

Apology and Request for Reconciliation

Dear [Recipient's Name],

I hope this email finds you well. I am writing to express my sincerest apologies for any role I might have played in the recent conflict between us.

Upon reflection, I realize that my actions or words may have contributed to the misunderstanding. I genuinely regret any inconvenience or discomfort this might have caused.

I value our professional relationship and believe that open communication and mutual respect are the cornerstones of a successful partnership. I am committed to learning from this experience and working towards a resolution that fosters a positive and collaborative working environment.

If you are open to it, I would like to discuss this matter further in person or via a call. I am eager to listen to your perspective and find a way to move forward together.

Once again, please accept my heartfelt apologies. I hope we can reconcile our differences and continue working together harmoniously.

Thank you for your understanding.

Warm regards,

[Your Name]

[Your Title/Position]

[Your Contact Information]

V4. *Mediation Request* (#060)

Request for Mediation

Dear [Recipient's Name],

I hope this email finds you well. In light of recent conflicts or misunderstandings that have arisen between us, I believe it would be beneficial to involve a neutral third party to facilitate open communication and reach a resolution.

I propose that we engage in mediation with the help of a professional mediator who can objectively guide us through the discussion. Mediation allows all parties to express their concerns and work towards a mutually agreeable solution.

I understand that engaging in mediation might require time and effort, but restoring harmony and strengthening our professional relationship is a worthwhile investment.

If you agree, I can research and provide recommendations for qualified mediators who can assist us.

Thank you for considering this proposal. I hope we can find a positive path forward through mediation.

Best regards,

[Your Name]

[Your Title/Position]

[Your Contact Information]

V5. Seeking Feedback for Resolution (#061)

Seeking Your Feedback for Resolution

Dear [Recipient's Name],

I hope this email finds you well. I am reaching out to address a recent conflict or misunderstanding that has occurred between us.

I genuinely value your input and perspective, and I believe that hearing your feedback is vital to finding a fair and satisfactory resolution for all parties involved.

If you are comfortable sharing your thoughts on the matter, I would be grateful to know your viewpoint. Please feel free to express any concerns or suggestions, as I am committed to fully understanding your position.

Once I understand your perspective, I will do my utmost to find a solution that addresses the issue at hand while preserving the mutual respect and professionalism that define our working relationship.

Thank you for your willingness to participate in this process. Your feedback is essential, and I am confident we can find a positive way forward together.

Sincerely,

[Your Name]

[Your Title/Position]

[Your Contact Information]

Making Persuasive Arguments or Proposals

Making persuasive arguments or proposals in your emails is essential for achieving your desired outcomes. Here are some tips to help you craft compelling and persuasive messages:

Understand Your Audience: Before making your argument or proposal, thoroughly understand your audience's needs, preferences, and pain points. Tailor your message to resonate with their interests and show how your proposal addresses their specific concerns.

Start Strong: Grab your reader's attention from the beginning. Use a powerful subject line and an opening sentence highlighting your proposal's benefits or value. Make the reader want to keep reading.

Present a Clear Value Proposition: Clearly state the benefits and advantages of your proposal. Explain how it solves a problem or fulfills a need better than other alternatives. Use data, evidence, and real-life examples to support your claims.

Use Persuasive Language: Choose your words carefully to create a sense of urgency and importance. Use positive and action-oriented language. Emphasize your proposal's positive impact on the recipient's business or life.

Address Potential Objections: Anticipate your audience's objections and address them in your email. Show that you've thought about potential concerns and have valid solutions.

Include Supporting Evidence: Back up your arguments with facts, statistics, case studies, testimonials, or other forms of evidence. This adds credibility to your proposal and builds trust with the recipient.

Appeal to Emotions: Emotions frequently sway people. Connect emotionally with your audience by sharing stories, anecdotes, or testimonials that evoke positive feelings about your proposal.

Be Concise and Organized: Keep your email focused and to the point. Use a clear and logical structure to present your arguments. Avoid unnecessary details that may distract from your main points.

Offer a Call to Action: End your email with a clear call to action. Clearly state what you want the recipient to do next, whether it's scheduling a meeting, providing feedback, or taking any specific action related to your proposal.

Follow Up: Don't be discouraged if you don't receive a response initially. Follow up on your email politely, reaffirming the value of your proposal and expressing your eagerness to discuss it further.

Be Professional and Courteous: Maintain a professional tone throughout the email. Be respectful, courteous, and appreciative of the recipient's time and consideration. Also, before hitting the send button, thoroughly proofread your email for grammar, spelling, and formatting errors. A well-written email enhances your credibility and professionalism.

By following these strategies, you can create persuasive arguments and proposals that are compelling, influential, and more likely to elicit the desired response from your recipients. Remember that persuasive communication is an art that improves with practice, so continue to refine your skills through experience and feedback.

Templates

V1. Product/Service Proposal (#062)

Introducing [Your Product/Service] - Elevate Your [Recipient's Company Name] Results

Dear [Recipient's Name],

I hope this email finds you well. I am writing to introduce you to an exciting opportunity that can significantly enhance [Recipient's Company Name]'s performance and deliver exceptional results.

[Your Product/Service] is a cutting-edge solution designed to address the specific challenges [Recipient's Company Name] is facing. With its user-friendly interface and innovative features, our product/service can streamline your processes, increase efficiency, and boost overall productivity.

Key Benefits of [Your Product/Service]:

- Benefit 1: [Highlight the primary advantage]
- Benefit 2: [Emphasize another valuable benefit]
- Benefit 3: [Mention the third significant benefit]

We have successfully helped numerous companies like [Case Study 1] and [Case Study 2] achieve remarkable growth and success in their respective industries.

I would like to schedule a brief meeting to demonstrate how [Your Product/Service] can specifically cater to [Recipient's Company Name]'s needs and answer any questions you may have.

Please let me know your availability for a call next week. I am confident that together, we can propel [Recipient's Company Name] towards unprecedented success.

Thank you for your time, and I look forward to discussing this exciting proposal further.

Best regards,

[Your Name]

[Your Title/Position]

[Your Company]

[Your Contact Information]

V2. Project Proposal (#063)

[Project Name] - Empowering [Recipient's Company Name] to Reach New Heights

Dear [Recipient's Name],

I hope this email finds you in good spirits. I am excited to present a comprehensive project proposal that has the potential to transform [Recipient's Company Name]'s operations and deliver remarkable outcomes.

Our proposed [Project Name] aims to address critical challenges and capitalize on growth opportunities to achieve the following key objectives:

1. Objective 1: [Clearly state the first objective]

2. Objective 2: [Clearly state the second objective]
3. Objective 3: [Clearly state the third objective]

Implementing [Project Name] will optimize efficiency and improve [Recipient's Company Name's] competitive edge within the industry. With our team of seasoned experts and a proven track record of successful projects, we are confident in our ability to deliver exceptional results.

We would be delighted to meet with you to present the details of our proposal, discuss timelines, and address any inquiries you may have. Please suggest a date and time that works best for you, and we will ensure that our team is available accordingly.

Thank you for considering our proposal. We are eager to embark on this transformative journey with [Recipient's Company Name].

Best regards,

[Your Name]

[Your Title/Position]

[Your Company]

[Your Contact Information]

V3. Partnership Proposal (#064)

Collaborate for Mutual Growth - Joint Venture Opportunity

Dear [Recipient's Name],

I hope this email finds you thriving in your endeavors. I am writing to explore an exciting partnership opportunity that can result in mutual growth and success for both our organizations.

[Your Company Name] and [Recipient's Company Name] share a common vision and complementary strengths that, when combined, can create unparalleled value in the market. Together, we can capitalize on the following advantages:

1. Advantage 1: [Explain the first advantage of the partnership]
2. Advantage 2: [Highlight the second advantage of the partnership]
3. Advantage 3: [Emphasize the third advantage of the partnership]

By leveraging our resources, expertise, and networks, we can reach new markets, enhance product offerings, and increase market share significantly.

I propose we schedule a meeting to discuss the finer details of this partnership and explore potential collaboration opportunities. Your insights and input are essential to the success of this venture.

Please let me know your availability, and I will gladly arrange a call at your convenience.

Thank you for considering this proposal. I look forward to exploring the possibilities of working together.

Warm regards,

[Your Name]

[Your Title/Position]

[Your Company]

[Your Contact Information]

V4. Salary Increment Request (#065)

Request for Salary Review - Reflecting Dedication and Accomplishments

Dear [Recipient's Name],

I hope this email finds you well. I am writing to discuss the possibility of a salary review in light of my unwavering dedication and significant contributions to [Your Company].

Over the past [duration], I have consistently exceeded performance targets and played a crucial role in [mention specific achievements or projects]. My commitment to [Your Company's] success and willingness to go above and beyond is reflected in the following accomplishments:

- Accomplishment 1: [Describe a notable achievement]
- Accomplishment 2: [Mention another significant contribution]
- Accomplishment 3: [Highlight an additional impact on the company]

Considering the exceptional value I bring to [Your Company], I kindly request a fair and deserved salary adjustment. I have thoroughly researched market rates for similar positions, and I believe my revised compensation should align with industry standards.

I would appreciate the opportunity to discuss this matter further in a meeting. Please let me know when you are available, and I will arrange a time that suits you best.

Thank you for considering my request. Your support in recognizing my efforts will undoubtedly strengthen my commitment to the continued success of [Your Company].

Sincerely,

[Your Name]

[Your Title/Position]

[Your Department]

[Your Contact Information]

Handling Complaints or Dissatisfied Customers

Handling complaints or dissatisfied customers via email requires a strategic approach that promptly, empathetically, and professionally addresses the customer's concerns. Here are some tips to effectively handle complaints or dissatisfied customers:

Respond Promptly: Acknowledge the complaint and respond as soon as possible. Delayed responses can escalate the issue and lead to further dissatisfaction. Aim to reply within 24 hours, if possible.

Show Empathy: Begin your email by expressing genuine empathy and understanding for the customer's situation. Let them know that you value their feedback and that their satisfaction is a top priority for your company.

Stay Calm and Professional: Maintain a calm and professional tone throughout the email. Avoid responding emotionally, even if the customer's complaint is aggressive or emotional. Stick to the facts and focus on finding a resolution.

Thank Them for Their Feedback: Thank the customer for bringing the issue to your attention. Viewing complaints as opportunities to improve your products or services can help turn a negative experience into a positive one.

Apologize Sincerely: Offer a sincere apology for any inconvenience or dissatisfaction the customer has experienced. Taking responsibility, even if your company didn't directly cause the issue, shows you care about their experience.

Listen Carefully: Carefully read and understand the customer's concerns. Address each specific point they raise in your response to demonstrate that you've taken the time to consider their feedback.

Investigate and Offer Solutions: Investigate the issue thoroughly before responding. If possible, explain what happened clearly and offer practical solutions to resolve the problem. Be transparent about any steps you'll take to prevent similar issues in the future.

Provide Contact Information: Offer your contact information or a dedicated customer support email address, so the customer can follow up if needed. Make it easy for them to reach out to you directly with any additional questions or concerns.

Offer Compensation (if appropriate): Consider offering compensation or a gesture of goodwill depending on the severity of the issue. This could be a discount on a future purchase or a replacement for a faulty product.

End Positively: Conclude the email on a positive note, reiterating your commitment to resolving the matter and ensuring their satisfaction. Invite them to contact you again if they need further assistance. Also, consider sending a follow-up email to ensure the customer is satisfied with the outcome. This extra step shows that you genuinely care about their experience.

Remember, handling complaints effectively can turn dissatisfied customers into loyal advocates for your business. Each interaction is an opportunity to showcase excellent customer service and build lasting relationships with your clientele.

Templates

V1. Acknowledging the Complaint (#066)

Acknowledgment of Your Concern

Dear [Customer's Name],

I hope this email finds you well. I am writing to acknowledge the concerns you raised in your recent message. Your feedback is essential to us, and we take your satisfaction seriously.

We apologize for any inconvenience caused and want to assure you that we are already looking into the matter. Our team is dedicated to resolving the issue promptly and to your satisfaction. We appreciate your patience as we investigate the situation thoroughly.

Once we have a resolution, we will contact you directly to discuss our steps to address your concerns. Your satisfaction is our top priority, and we are committed to ensuring that you have a positive experience with us.

Thank you for bringing this matter to our attention. If you have any additional information or questions, please don't hesitate to reach out to us.

Sincerely,

[Your Name]

[Your Title]

[Your Company]

V2. Apologizing and Offering a Solution (#067)

Apology and Resolution for Your Concern

Dear [Customer's Name],

I sincerely apologize for the inconvenience you experienced with our [product/service]. Your feedback is invaluable, and we are committed to rectifying the situation promptly.

Upon investigating the matter, we have identified the issue and are taking immediate steps to correct it. We are offering [specific solution, e.g., a refund, replacement, discount, etc.] to compensate for the inconvenience. Please be assured that we are implementing measures to prevent the recurrence of such issues in the future.

Your satisfaction is paramount to us, and we want to regain your trust in our brand. We genuinely appreciate your business and value your feedback as it helps us improve our products/services.

If you have any further concerns or questions, please don't hesitate to reach out to us. We are here to assist you in any way we can.

Thank you for giving us the opportunity to resolve this matter. We look forward to serving you better in the future.

Sincerely,

[Your Name]

[Your Title]

[Your Company]

V3. *Addressing Product/Service Quality Issues* (#068)

Resolution for Product/Service Quality Concerns

Dear [Customer's Name],

Thank you for bringing your concerns about the quality of our [product/service] to our attention. We understand the importance of delivering exceptional products/services and sincerely apologize for the disappointment caused.

Rest assured, we take your feedback seriously and have already begun investigating the matter. Our quality control team is conducting a thorough assessment to identify any lapses and implement necessary improvements.

In the meantime, we would like to offer you a replacement [product/service] of your choice or a full refund. Please let us know your preference, and we will proceed accordingly.

Once again, we apologize for any inconvenience and appreciate your understanding. Your satisfaction remains our priority, and we are committed to restoring your faith in our brand.

If there is anything else we can do to assist you further, please don't hesitate to reach out to us.

Sincerely,

[Your Name]

[Your Title]

[Your Company]

V4. Handling Service-related Complaints (#069)

Resolution for Service-related Concerns

Dear [Customer's Name],

I want to extend my sincere apologies for the unsatisfactory service you experienced during your recent visit to our [store/office/branch]. Your feedback is crucial to us, and we deeply regret that we fell short of your expectations.

I have personally reviewed your case, and we are taking immediate steps to address the issues you encountered. Our team is undergoing additional training to improve our service standards, and we are implementing measures to prevent similar occurrences in the future.

To express our commitment to providing exceptional service, we would like to offer you [specific compensation, e.g., a gift card, a complimentary service, etc.] for your next visit. Please accept this gesture of goodwill as a token of our appreciation for your patience and understanding.

We genuinely value your business and would like to assure you that we are dedicated to delivering a seamless and delightful experience during your next visit.

If you have any further questions or concerns, please do not hesitate to contact me directly at [your email/phone]. Thank you for giving us the opportunity to address this matter, and we hope to welcome you back soon.

Sincerely,

[Your Name]

[Your Title]

[Your Company]

V5. Handling Communication or Shipping Issues (#070)

Resolution for Communication/Shipping Concerns

Dear [Customer's Name],

I want to personally apologize for the communication/shipping issues you encountered with your recent order. Your satisfaction is essential to us, and we deeply regret any inconvenience this may have caused.

After investigating the matter, we have identified the problem's root cause and taken corrective actions. To prevent similar issues in the future, we are enhancing our internal processes to ensure smoother communication and more reliable shipping.

Regarding your order, we have expedited the shipment, and you can expect it to arrive at your doorstep within the next [specific timeframe, e.g., 1-2 business days].

As a gesture of goodwill, we would like to offer you [specific compensation, e.g., free shipping on your next order, a discount on your next purchase, etc.]. Your loyalty is invaluable to us, and we want to show our appreciation for your patience and understanding.

If you have any further questions or concerns, please do not hesitate to contact our customer support team at [customer support email/phone number]. We are here to assist you and ensure your satisfaction.

Thank you for giving us the opportunity to address this matter. We look forward to serving you better in the future.

Sincerely,

[Your Name]

[Your Title]

[Your Company]

Negotiating Contracts or Agreements

Effective negotiation is about getting what you want and finding a mutually beneficial solution. Using a clear, professional, and collaborative approach in your negotiation emails can increase the likelihood of successful contract agreements and strengthen your business relationships. Negotiating contracts or agreements via email requires finesse, clarity, and a strategic approach. Here are some key tips to excel in negotiating contracts or agreements through email:

Establish Rapport: Begin by building a positive relationship with the recipient. Use a friendly and professional tone in your initial email to create a collaborative atmosphere for the negotiation process.

Clearly State the Purpose: In the opening of your email, clearly state the purpose of the negotiation. Be specific about what you are seeking or proposing, whether it's terms, conditions, pricing, or other elements of the contract.

Highlight Mutual Benefits: Emphasize the mutual benefits of the proposed contract. Show the recipient how the agreement will be advantageous to both parties and address any potential concerns they may have.

Organize Your Points: Present your negotiation points in a well-organized manner. Use bullet points or numbered lists to make it easier for the recipient to understand and respond to each item separately.

Support with Data: When possible, back up your negotiation points with data, market research, or industry benchmarks. Providing evidence will strengthen your arguments and demonstrate your preparedness.

Be Flexible: Negotiations often involve give-and-take. Be open to compromise and demonstrate flexibility where appropriate. This willingness to find common ground can lead to more successful outcomes.

Address Concerns: Anticipate and address potential concerns or objections the recipient might have. Show empathy and offer solutions to alleviate their worries.

Avoid Aggressive Language: Maintain a professional and respectful tone throughout the negotiation. Avoid using aggressive or confrontational language, as it can lead to misunderstandings or escalate tensions.

Include Specific Details: Be clear and specific about any terms, conditions, or timelines you are proposing. Vague language can lead to confusion and hinder the negotiation process.

Request Confirmation: End your email by requesting confirmation of receipt and acknowledging the recipient's willingness to engage in the negotiation. This encourages a response and shows that you value their input.

Be Prompt and Courteous: Respond to any emails from the recipient promptly and courteously. A timely response shows you are engaged and committed to the negotiation process.

Summarize Agreements: As the negotiation progresses and agreements are reached, summarize the key points in subsequent emails. This helps to ensure that both parties are on the same page and minimizes misunderstandings.

Templates

V1. Initial Proposal Email (#071)

Proposal for Contract Negotiation - [Your Company Name]

Dear [Recipient's Name],

I hope this email finds you well. We are excited about the prospect of working together and believe collaboration between [Your Name] and [Recipient's Company Name] will be mutually beneficial.

We have thoroughly reviewed the proposed contract/agreement and appreciate the effort put into it. Before we proceed further, we would like to propose a few modifications to ensure that the terms align better with our requirements and objectives.

[Include specific points of negotiation or requested changes]

We understand the importance of reaching an agreement that works for both parties and is open to further discussions. Please let us know your thoughts on these proposed modifications, and we are eager to find common ground for a successful partnership.

Looking forward to your response and the opportunity to finalize the agreement together.

Best regards,

[Your Name]

[Your Title/Position]

[Your Company Name]

[Contact Information]

V2. Counter-Offer Email (#072)

Counter-Offer for Contract Negotiation - [Your Company Name]

Dear [Recipient's Name],

Thank you for your swift response to our initial proposal. We appreciate the progress made so far in the contract negotiation process.

After careful consideration, we have reviewed the proposed amendments and would like to present our counter-offer for your review and discussion:

[Include specific points of negotiation or counter-offer]

We believe these revisions better align with our business goals while maintaining a fair and balanced agreement between our organizations. Our aim is to ensure a successful partnership that serves the interests of both parties.

We are open to further dialogue to reach a consensus and are confident that we can find a solution that meets both of our needs.

Please let us know your thoughts on these proposed changes. We are eager to work together towards a mutually agreeable contract.

Thank you for your attention to this matter.

Sincerely,

[Your Name]

[Your Title/Position]

[Your Company Name]

[Contact Information]

V3. Finalizing Agreement Email (#073)

Finalizing Contract - [Your Company Name]

Dear [Recipient's Name],

We are pleased to see that our negotiations have led to significant progress, and we are now close to finalizing the agreement between [Your Company Name] and [Recipient's Company Name].

After considering all the points of discussion, we believe we have reached a comprehensive and mutually beneficial contract.

Before proceeding with the final signing, I kindly request that you review the attached contract again and confirm that all the agreed-upon changes have been accurately incorporated.

If everything aligns with your expectations, please provide us with your final approval, and we can move forward to formalize the agreement.

We value the opportunity to work together and are excited about the prospects of this partnership.

Thank you for your cooperation.

Best regards,

[Your Name]

[Your Title/Position]

[Your Company Name]

[Contact Information]

V4. Agreement Rejection with Counter-Proposal Email (#074)

Re: Contract Negotiation - [Your Company Name]

Dear [Recipient's Name],

Thank you for the updated contract proposal. We have carefully reviewed the changes you suggested and have some concerns that we believe need to be addressed for us to move forward with the agreement.

We appreciate the effort put into this contract and understand that it represents your company's interests. However, we feel that certain clauses need further clarification or adjustments to align with our business goals.

[Explain the reasons for the rejection and present specific counter-proposals]

We value the potential collaboration between our companies and are optimistic that we can find common ground. Our aim is to establish a mutually beneficial and fair agreement.

Please take some time to review our counter-proposals, and we are eager to discuss any further suggestions you may have.

Looking forward to your response.

Best regards,

[Your Name]

[Your Title/Position]

[Your Company Name]

[Contact Information]

V5. Agreement Acceptance and Appreciation Email (#075)

Re: Finalizing Contract - [Your Company Name]

Dear [Your Name],

I am pleased to confirm that we have reviewed the final contract, and it meets our expectations and requirements. We are delighted to accept the proposed terms and proceed with the partnership between [Your Company Name] and [Recipient's Company Name].

Thank you for your patience and flexibility throughout the negotiation process. We believe this agreement reflects a fair and mutually advantageous collaboration that will pave the way for our shared success.

We look forward to working closely with your team and achieving our common objectives.

Kind regards,

[Recipient's Name]

[Recipient's Title/Position]

[Recipient's Company Name]

[Contact Information]

Conducting Performance Reviews or Feedback

Conducting performance reviews or providing feedback via email requires a thoughtful and professional approach. It is essential to fostering a productive and positive work environment. Providing thoughtful and constructive feedback via email can help employees grow and develop, contributing to the business's overall success. Here are some tips to ensure your feedback is effective and well-received:

Choose the Right Time and Format: Ensure you conduct performance reviews or deliver feedback appropriately. Avoid sending critical feedback via email during high-stress periods or busy workdays. Use a formal and respectful email format for performance reviews, using a proper subject line that indicates the purpose of the email.

Be Specific and Objective: Provide specific examples of the employee's performance or behavior to make your feedback more meaningful. Use objective language, focusing on observable actions rather than personal characteristics. This helps the recipient understand exactly what areas need improvement or what they are doing well.

Balance Positive and Constructive Feedback: When conducting performance reviews, strike a balance between highlighting achievements and offering areas for improvement. Incorporate positive feedback to recognize accomplishments and show appreciation for the employee's efforts. This can motivate the individual to work on areas that need improvement.

Use the "SBI" Model for Constructive Feedback: Use the "Situation-Behavior-Impact" model when giving constructive feedback. Describe the specific situation, the observed behavior, and the impact of that behavior on the team or the project. This approach helps the recipient understand the consequences of their actions and provides a clear path for improvement.

Offer Guidance and Support: In your feedback email, offer guidance and support to help the employee improve. Suggest actionable steps they can take to address any shortcomings and achieve their goals. Reinforce your willingness to provide support and resources as needed.

Be Respectful and Empathetic: Show empathy and respect when delivering feedback. Avoid using harsh or confrontational language, as it may lead to a defensive response. Instead, be diplomatic and use a tone that encourages open communication.

Encourage Two-Way Communication: Invite employees to share their thoughts and perspectives on the feedback received. Encouraging open dialogue allows for more constructive exchange and demonstrates that you value their input.

Avoid Using Negative Language: Refrain from using negative language or making personal attacks. Focus on the behavior or performance rather than making it a personal issue. Constructive criticism should be about improving performance, not demoralizing the individual.

End on a Positive Note: Conclude the email on a positive and supportive note. Reiterate your belief in the employee's potential and express your confidence in their ability to improve and grow professionally.

Follow-up in Person: If possible, arrange a follow-up meeting in person or via video conference to discuss the feedback further. This allows for a more comprehensive discussion and the opportunity to address any concerns or questions the recipient may have.

Templates

V1. General Performance Review Template (#076)

Performance Review—[Employee Name]

Dear [Employee's Name],

I hope this email finds you well. I would like to conduct a performance review with you as part of our ongoing commitment to employee growth and development. Your dedication and contributions to the team have been valuable, and we believe this review will provide an opportunity to discuss your accomplishments and set goals for the future.

Let's schedule a meeting at your earliest convenience. During our meeting, we will cover the following topics:

1. Review your key achievements and strengths during the review period.
2. Areas where we see opportunities for improvement and development.
3. Your professional goals and aspirations.
4. Support and resources available to help you succeed.

Please come prepared to discuss your accomplishments and challenges openly. We value your input and look forward to a constructive conversation.

Kindly suggest a few dates and times that work for you, and I'll confirm the meeting accordingly.

Best regards,

[Your Name]

[Your Title/Department]

[Company Name]

[Contact Information]

V2. Positive Performance Feedback Template (#077)

Appreciation for Outstanding Performance

Dear [Employee's Name],

I wanted to take a moment to acknowledge your exceptional performance and dedication to your role. Your hard work and commitment have been exemplary, and your positive impact on the team and company are evident.

You consistently exceed expectations in [specific areas], and your ability to [mention a specific achievement or skill] has been invaluable to our success.

Thank you for your continuous efforts and for setting a high standard for your peers. Your contributions do not go unnoticed, and we genuinely appreciate your commitment to excellence.

Keep up the fantastic work!

Best regards,

[Your Name]

[Your Title/Department]

[Company Name]

[Contact Information]

V3. Improvement Feedback Template (#078)

Feedback and Growth Opportunities

Dear [Employee's Name],

I hope you're doing well. As part of our commitment to supporting your professional growth, I'd like to discuss a few areas where we see opportunities for improvement.

During the recent review period, we noticed [mention specific areas where improvement is needed]. While your dedication is commendable, addressing these areas will help you achieve even greater success in your role.

Let's schedule a meeting to discuss these points further and explore ways we can provide you with the necessary support and resources.

Remember, we are here to help you succeed, and addressing areas of improvement is a natural part of professional growth.

Please let me know your availability for a meeting.

Best regards,

[Your Name]

[Your Title/Department]

[Company Name]

[Contact Information]

V4. Goal Setting and Development Template (#079)

Setting Goals for Growth and Development

Dear [Employee's Name],

I hope this email finds you well. As we approach the end of the review period, I would like to discuss your professional goals and aspirations for the upcoming months.

Your achievements and commitment to the team have been notable, and we believe that setting clear goals will help you stay on track and continue to excel in your role.

In our meeting, we'll focus on the following:

1. Review your accomplishments during the review period.

2. Discussion of your career goals and aspirations.
3. Setting specific and measurable objectives for the next review period.
4. Identification of any training or development opportunities to support your growth.

Your input and perspective are essential, and we look forward to a productive conversation.

Kindly suggest a few dates and times that work for you, and I'll confirm the meeting accordingly.

Best regards,

[Your Name]

[Your Title/Department]

[Company Name]

[Contact Information]

V5. Encouraging Feedback Template (#080)

Feedback and Your Valuable Input

Dear [Employee's Name],

I hope you are doing well. We highly value your contribution to our team and the company, and we believe your perspective is essential to our success.

As part of our commitment to fostering an open and inclusive environment, we encourage you to share any feedback, suggestions, or ideas about our team's operations, processes, or initiatives.

Your input is valuable; we want to ensure your voice is heard. Please feel free to share your thoughts with us; we're more than willing to listen and consider your insights.

Thank you for being an integral part of our team, and we look forward to hearing from you.

Best regards,

[Your Name]

[Your Title/Department]

[Company Name]

[Contact Information]

Communicating Bad News or Layoffs

Communicating bad news or layoffs is a sensitive task that requires compassion and understanding. As an email expert, your expertise lies in crafting messages that convey difficult information while maintaining professionalism and empathy. Communicating bad news or layoffs via business email requires sensitivity, clarity, and empathy. Here are some essential tips for effectively conveying such challenging messages:

Be Transparent and Timely: Deliver the bad news or layoff information as soon as possible. Delaying communication can create anxiety and uncertainty. Choose an appropriate email time, considering the recipient's time zone and work schedule.

Choose the Right Tone: While it's essential to remain professional, show empathy and understanding in your tone. Acknowledge the difficulty of the situation and express appreciation for the recipient's contributions.

Begin with Empathy: Start the email by expressing empathy and acknowledging the emotions the news might evoke. Show that you understand the impact this news may have on the recipient and the organization as a whole. Also, clearly and concisely explain the reasons behind the bad news or layoff. Use straightforward language without being overly technical or jargon-heavy.

Offer Support and Resources: If applicable, provide information on resources available to affected employees, such as severance packages, outplacement services, or counseling support.

Address Questions and Concerns: Anticipate that recipients will have questions and concerns. Encourage them to reach out for further clarification or support and provide contact information for relevant HR representatives or managers.

Maintain Confidentiality: If necessary, remind recipients of the need to maintain confidentiality about the information shared in the email until the official announcement is made.

Avoid Blaming or Guilt: Refrain from blaming individuals or creating feelings of guilt. Instead, focus on the larger organizational or economic factors that led to the decision.

End on a Positive Note: Conclude the email positively and encouragingly. Express gratitude for the recipient's contributions and offer well wishes for their future endeavors.

Consider the Format: Consider whether a personal email or group announcement is more suitable depending on the circumstances and the number of recipients. In the case of layoffs, individual emails might be more thoughtful and compassionate.

Templates

V1. Bad News to a Customer (#081)

Update on [Product/Service] Delivery

Dear [Customer's Name],

I hope this email finds you well. I am writing to inform you about an unexpected delay in the delivery of [Product/Service]. Unfortunately, due to unforeseen circumstances beyond our control, we are experiencing delays in the production process.

We understand the inconvenience this may cause, and we sincerely apologize for any inconvenience this delay may have caused you. Our team is working diligently to resolve the issue and expedite the delivery as much as possible. Your satisfaction is of the utmost importance to us, and we assure you that we are doing everything in our capacity to rectify the situation.

Once again, we apologize for the inconvenience and truly appreciate your understanding. If you have any questions or concerns, please do not hesitate to reach out to our customer support team at [Customer Support Contact].

Thank you for your patience and continued support.

Best regards,

[Your Name]

[Your Title/Position]

[Company Name]

[Contact Information]

V2. Layoff Announcement to Employees (#082)

Important Update from [Company Name]

Dear [Employee's Name],

I hope this message finds you well. I am writing to inform you about the company's challenging decision. After careful consideration and in response to the current economic conditions, we have had to make the difficult decision to implement a workforce reduction.

Unfortunately, this means that your position at [Company Name] will be affected, and we must regretfully inform you that your employment with the company will be terminated, effective [Last Working Date]. Please be assured that this decision was not taken lightly, and it is in no way a reflection of your dedication and hard work.

We understand that this news may be upsetting, and we are committed to supporting you during this transition. Our HR team will be available to provide information on severance packages, benefits continuation, and other resources available to assist you in your job search.

I want to personally thank you for your valuable contributions to [Company Name]. Your dedication and efforts have been highly appreciated and have contributed significantly to our team's success.

If you have any questions or need further assistance, please don't hesitate to reach out to HR at [HR Contact Information].

Wishing you all the best in your future endeavors.

Sincerely,

[Your Name]

[Your Title/Position]

[Company Name]

[Contact Information]

V3. Bad News Regarding Project Delays (#083)

Update on [Project Name] Timeline

Dear [Recipient's Name],

I hope this email finds you well. I am writing to provide you with an update on the progress of [Project Name].

Regrettably, we have encountered unforeseen challenges during the project implementation, which have resulted in unavoidable delays. As a result, we anticipate that the project's completion date will be extended by [X] weeks/months.

Please know that our team is working diligently to address these challenges and expedite the project while ensuring the highest quality results. We understand the importance of this project to you and our organization, and we sincerely apologize for any inconvenience these delays may cause.

We will inform you of further developments and provide regular progress updates. If you have any questions or concerns, please feel free to reach out to me directly.

Thank you for your understanding and continued support.

Best regards,

[Your Name]

[Your Title/Position]

[Company Name]

[Contact Information]

V4. Bad News Regarding Service Disruption(#084)

Notice of Service Disruption

Dear [Customer's Name],

We hope this message finds you well. We regret to inform you that there will be a temporary disruption in [Service Name] starting from [Start Date] until [End Date]. This disruption is due to necessary maintenance and upgrades essential to enhance our service's overall performance and reliability.

While we understand the inconvenience this may cause, we assure you that our team is working diligently to minimize the duration of the disruption. We apologize for any inconvenience this may cause and appreciate your patience and understanding.

If you have any urgent matters during this period, don't hesitate to contact our customer support team at [Customer Support Contact].

Thank you for your continued support and cooperation.

Sincerely,

[Your Name]

[Your Title/Position]

[Company Name]

[Contact Information]

V5. Bad News Regarding Contract Termination (#085)

Termination of [Contract/Service] Agreement

Dear [Recipient's Name],

I hope you are doing well. I am writing to inform you that, unfortunately, we have made the difficult decision to terminate the [Contract/Service] agreement between [Your Company Name] and [Recipient's Company Name]. The termination will be effective as of [Termination Date].

This decision was not taken lightly and is based on [Explain the reason for termination, such as performance issues, budget constraints, or strategic changes]. Please know that we value our business relationship with [Recipient's Company Name] and have carefully considered all options before reaching this conclusion.

We want to express our appreciation for your trust in us and our opportunities to work together. During the transition period, our team will work closely with you to ensure a smooth handover and to address any outstanding matters.

If you have any questions or concerns regarding the termination or the transition process, please do not hesitate to reach out to me directly.

Thank you for your understanding and cooperation.

Best regards,

[Your Name]

[Your Title/Position]

[Your Company Name]

[Contact Information]

Requesting Time Off

Requesting time off is an essential part of professional communication, and it involves formally asking for permission to be absent from work for a specified period. Whether it's for personal reasons, vacations, medical appointments, or any other legitimate purpose, employees should follow certain guidelines when crafting a time-off request email to maintain professionalism and ensure a smooth workflow within the organization. Here's an elaborate explanation of the process:

Request Purpose: State the purpose of your email right away by mentioning that you are requesting time off. Be specific about the dates or duration for which you wish to be absent. Include the start and end dates to avoid any confusion.

Reason for Request: It's a good practice to provide a brief reason for your time-off request. However, you do not need to disclose personal details if you're uncomfortable doing so. A general reason, such as "I need to take care of a personal matter" or "I have a planned family vacation," should suffice.

Availability and Work Coverage: Demonstrate your professionalism by addressing how your responsibilities will be handled during your absence. Offer to complete pending tasks or delegate them to a colleague. If necessary, propose a plan for work coverage to minimize any disruptions caused by your absence.

Gratitude and Politeness: Express gratitude for considering your request and understanding the impact it might have on the team or project. Use polite language throughout the email, maintaining a positive tone.

Contact Information: Provide your contact information, such as your phone number or an alternative email, in case of any urgent matters that may require your attention during your absence.

Attachments (if necessary): If your company requires any specific time-off request forms or documents, attach them to the email to expedite the approval process.

Follow-Up: If you don't receive a response to your time-off request within a reasonable time frame, politely follow up with a brief and friendly reminder.

Templates

V1. Standard Time Off Request (#086)

Time Off Request

Dear [Manager's Name],

I hope this email finds you well. I am writing to formally request time off from work for [number of days] starting from [start date] to [end date]. I will be taking [personal/vacation/medical] leave during this period.

I have ensured that all my pending tasks are up to date, and I will make sure to delegate any critical responsibilities to my colleagues. I am confident that my absence will not significantly impact ongoing projects or team productivity.

Please let me know if there is any specific process I need to follow for the time off request or if there are any additional details you require from me.

Thank you for considering my request. I am looking forward to your approval and appreciate your understanding.

Best regards,

[Your Name]

[Your Job Title]

V2. Emergency Time Off Request (#087)

Urgent Time Off Request

Dear [Manager's Name],

I hope this email finds you well. Unfortunately, I am facing an unexpected family emergency that requires my immediate attention. As such, I need to request [number of days] of emergency time off starting from [start date] to [end date].

I understand the urgency of the situation and assure you that I will do my best to address any critical tasks before my departure. I will also coordinate with my colleagues to ensure a smooth workflow during my absence.

I apologize for any inconvenience this may cause, and I appreciate your understanding and support during this challenging time.

Please let me know if there are any procedures I need to follow or any additional information you require.

Thank you for your prompt attention to this matter.

Sincerely,

[Your Name]

[Your Job Title]

V3. *Time Off Request for Personal Reasons* (#088)

Time Off Request for Personal Reasons

Dear [Manager's Name],

I hope this email finds you well. I am writing to request time off from work for [number of days] starting from [start date] to [end date]. The reason for my request is [provide a brief reason for your leave, e.g., attending a family event, addressing personal matters, etc.].

I have planned my tasks accordingly and will ensure all pending work is completed or appropriately delegated to my team members. I am committed to maintaining the highest level of productivity before and after my absence.

Please let me know if I need to follow any specific guidelines or procedures for the time off request.

Thank you for considering my request, and I am happy to discuss any further details if necessary.

Best regards,

[Your Name]

[Your Job Title]

SALES AND MARKETING EMAILS

S ales and marketing emails are essential for businesses to promote their products, services, and brand and engage with existing and potential customers. These types of emails are pivotal in driving revenue, building customer relationships, and establishing a strong market presence. Hence, understanding the art of crafting effective sales and marketing emails is crucial for maximizing business growth and success.

Sales emails are designed to generate interest, attract prospects, and convert leads into paying customers. On the other hand, marketing emails encompass a broader range of communication, including newsletters, promotional offers, product announcements, and content-driven campaigns. Both types of emails complement each other, working together to create a seamless and persuasive customer journey.

The key to successful sales and marketing emails lies in their ability to deliver value to the recipients while maintaining a personalized and authentic touch. These emails should cut through the clutter of the recipient's inbox, capture their attention, and provide compelling reasons to take the desired action.

In this age of digital communication, sales and marketing emails have evolved significantly, incorporating various strategies such as automation, personalization, A/B testing, and data-driven insights. By leveraging these techniques, businesses can optimize their email campaigns to deliver the right message, to the right audience, at the right time.

This chapter will discuss how to segment your email lists strategically, tailor your messages based on recipient preferences, and nurture leads through the sales funnel. By mastering the art of sales and marketing emails, you can build long-lasting relationships with your customers, foster brand loyalty, and achieve sustainable business growth.

Sales Email Templates

Sales emails are critical for businesses to connect with potential and existing customers, promote products or services, build relationships, and ultimately drive revenue growth. Businesses can significantly enhance their sales effectiveness and overall success by understanding the role of sales emails and implementing best practices for crafting compelling and personalized messages. Here are the key aspects of the role of sales emails:

Prospecting and Lead Generation: Sales emails are instrumental in identifying and reaching out to potential customers or leads. These emails are sent to prospects who have shown interest in the product or service offered by the company or have the potential to become valuable clients.

Building Relationships: Sales emails are about making a quick sale and building and nurturing relationships with prospects and existing customers. Successful sales emails aim to establish trust and credibility, fostering a long-term relationship that can lead to repeat business and referrals.

Introducing Products/Services: Sales emails serve as a platform to introduce and highlight the features and benefits of products or services. They explain how the offering addresses the recipient's pain points or fulfills their needs, making a compelling case for why they should consider the product.

Customization and Personalization: Effective sales emails are personalized to cater to the specific needs and interests of the recipient. Personalization demonstrates that the sender has taken the time to understand the prospect's requirements, increasing the chances of engagement.

Handling Objections: Sales emails are often used to address common objections or concerns that prospects may have. By proactively addressing potential reservations, sales professionals can build confidence in the product or service and overcome barriers to making a purchase.

Call-to-Action (CTA): A crucial element of a sales email is the call-to-action. This is a clear and direct request for the recipient to take a specific action, such as scheduling a demo, signing up for a trial, or making a purchase. A well-crafted CTA compels the recipient to take the desired step, moving them further along the sales funnel.

Follow-ups: Sales emails are instrumental in the follow-up process. After an initial contact or interaction, follow-up emails help maintain momentum and keep the prospect engaged with the sales process.

Tracking and Analytics: Sales emails can be tracked and analyzed to measure their effectiveness. Metrics such as open, click-through, and conversion rates provide valuable insights into the email campaign's success. This data can be used to refine email strategies and improve future outreach.

Upselling and Cross-selling: For existing customers, sales emails can be used to promote complementary products or services, leading to upselling or cross-selling opportunities. These emails leverage the existing relationship and trust built with the customer to expand the value of the transaction.

Automating Outreach: Sales emails can be automated using customer relationship management (CRM) software or email marketing platforms.

This automation streamlines the sales process, allowing sales professionals to reach many prospects while maintaining a personalized touch efficiently.

Templates

V1. Initial Sales Outreach (#089)

[Prospect's Name], [Your Company] Can Help You [Benefit]

Hi [Prospect's Name],

I hope this email finds you well. My name is [Your Name], and I'm reaching out from [Your Company]. We specialize in [briefly mention your product or service's benefits].

I noticed [mention a relevant trigger/event that caught your attention]. Based on your [company's recent news/blog post/social media activity], it seems like you might be interested in [related value proposition]. We've helped [mention a successful client or relevant industry statistic].

I'd love to set up a quick call to discuss how we can support your goals. Are you available for a 15-minute call next [suggest two date and time options]?

Looking forward to connecting with you.

Best regards,

[Your Name]

[Your Title]

[Your Company]

[Your Contact Information]

V2. Follow-up on Initial Sales Outreach (#090)

Re: [Your Last Email's Subject]

Hi [Prospect's Name],

I hope you're doing well. I wanted to follow up on my previous email to see if you had a chance to review it. We truly believe that [mention the value your product/service brings to the prospect's business].

If you have any questions or need further information, feel free to ask. I'm here to assist you throughout the process.

Let me know if you're available for a call to discuss this further. Looking forward to hearing from you.

Best regards,

[Your Name]

[Your Title]

[Your Company]

[Your Contact Information]

V3. Personalized Sales Offer (#091)

[Prospect's Name], Exclusive Offer Inside

Hi [Prospect's Name],

I hope this email finds you well. As a valued [industry/position] professional, I wanted to offer you an exclusive discount on our [product/service].

Our [product/service] is tailored to [mention the specific benefits relevant to the prospect]. This special offer is only available to a select few in the [industry/position], and I thought you might find it valuable for [prospect's specific business challenge/goal].

To take advantage of this limited-time offer, simply reply to this email or give me a call at [your phone number]. Let's discuss how [Your Company] can support your success.

Looking forward to hearing from you.

Best regards,

[Your Name]

[Your Title]

[Your Company]

[Your Contact Information]

V4. Reengagement Email (#092)

We Miss You at [Your Company]

Hi [Prospect's Name],

I hope this email finds you well. It's been a while since we last connected, and I wanted to reach out and see how things are going at [Prospect's Company].

At [Your Company], we are continually improving our offerings to better serve our clients. I wanted to extend an invitation for you to revisit our [product/service] and explore the new features and enhancements we've made.

Let's schedule a brief call to catch up and discuss how we can best support your needs. I have some exciting updates to share that I believe will be of interest to you.

Are you available for a quick call next [suggest two date and time options]?

Looking forward to reconnecting with you.

Best regards,

[Your Name]

[Your Title]

[Your Company]

[Your Contact Information]

V5. Follow-up on Meeting or Demo (#093)

Re: [Meeting/Demo Date] Recap and Next Steps

Hi [Prospect's Name],

I hope you found our [meeting/demo] valuable and informative. Thank you for taking the time to explore how [Your Company] can benefit your business.

As discussed, I've attached the [presentation/proposal] for your reference. Please feel free to reach out if you have any questions or require further clarification.

Additionally, I'd love to hear your thoughts on how our [product/service] aligns with your business goals. Let's schedule a follow-up call to discuss any concerns or explore the next steps.

Looking forward to continuing the conversation.

Best regards,

[Your Name]

[Your Title]

[Your Company]

[Your Contact Information]

V6. Customer Testimonial and Case Study (#094)

[Prospect's Name], See How [Client Name] Achieved [Result]

Hi [Prospect's Name],

I hope this email finds you well. I wanted to share a success story from one of our clients, [Client Name]. They faced similar challenges to what your company might be experiencing, and our [product/service] helped them achieve impressive results.

[Provide a brief overview of the client's challenge and how your solution addressed it]. You can read the full case study attached to this email.

I believe this case study demonstrates how our [product/service] can drive tangible benefits for businesses like yours. I'd love to discuss how we can tailor a solution to meet your specific needs.

When would be a good time to connect and explore this further?

Best regards,

[Your Name]

[Your Title]

[Your Company]

[Your Contact Information]

V7. Follow-up after Trial Period (#095)

Re: [Product/Service] Trial Expiring Soon

Hi [Prospect's Name],

I hope you've been enjoying your trial of [Your Company]'s [product/service]. We trust it has provided value to your business and demonstrated how it can enhance [specific benefits].

As your trial period is coming to an end on [Trial End Date], I wanted to check in and see if you have any questions or need further assistance. Our team is here to support your decision-making process.

If you want to continue with a full subscription or explore other options, I'd be happy to discuss pricing and plans that suit your business requirements.

Please let me know how you'd like to proceed.

Best regards,

[Your Name]

[Your Title]

[Your Company]

[Your Contact Information]

V8. Handling Objections (#096)

Addressing Your Concerns about [Product/Service]

Hi [Prospect's Name],

I hope this email finds you well. Thank you for expressing your concerns about our [product/service]. I appreciate your honest feedback and I'd like to address these points.

[Address the prospect's specific objections one by one]. Our team has worked diligently to ensure that our [product/service] provides a seamless experience and addresses your challenges.

We value your business, and I'd be more than happy to schedule a call to discuss any additional concerns or clarify how we've improved our offering.

Please let me know your availability, and we can further explore how our [product/service] aligns with your needs.

Best regards,

[Your Name]

[Your Title]

[Your Company]

[Your Contact Information]

V9. Time-Sensitive Offer (#097)

Exclusive [Product/Service] Discount Ends Soon

Hi [Prospect's Name],

I hope this email finds you well. I wanted to inform you that our exclusive discount on [product/service] is ending soon.

This limited-time offer can significantly benefit your business by [mention key value propositions]. Don't miss out on the chance to capitalize on this incredible deal.

Reach out to me at [your phone number] or reply to this email to secure your discounted rate. I'd be happy to discuss the details and help you get started.

Looking forward to assisting you.

Best

Regards,

[Your Name]

[Your Title]

[Your Company]

[Your Contact Information]

V10. Referral Request (#098)

[Prospect's Name], Can You Recommend Someone in Need of [Your Product/Service]?

Hi [Prospect's Name],

I hope all is well. I have a quick request. As a valued client, I know you've benefited from our [product/service].

If you know anyone in your network who might be interested in improving [mention benefits], would you be willing to introduce us? Your recommendation means a lot to us, and we'd be thrilled to offer them exceptional service.

Feel free to forward this email or share their contact information, and we'll take it from there.

Thank you for your support.

Best regards,

[Your Name]

[Your Title]

[Your Company]

[Your Contact Information]

Marketing Email Templates

Marketing emails are crucial to a company's overall marketing strategy and communication with its target audience. They serve as a direct and measurable way to communicate with customers, promote products, build brand loyalty, and drive business growth. These emails are a powerful tool for businesses to directly promote their products, services, events, and brand messages to potential and existing customers. When crafted strategically and delivered to the right audience, marketing emails can yield significant returns on investment and contribute to the overall success of a business. Below are the key roles and benefits of marketing emails:

Promoting Products and Services: One of the primary roles of marketing emails is to showcase new products or services, highlight their features and benefits, and persuade recipients to make a purchase. Marketing emails serve as a direct channel to present offerings to a targeted audience and stimulate interest in what the company offers.

Building Brand Awareness: Businesses can reinforce their brand identity and values through consistent and well-crafted marketing emails. By incorporating branded elements like logos, colors, and messaging, these emails help recipients recognize and recall the company, thus increasing brand awareness and familiarity.

Nurturing Leads: Marketing emails are instrumental in lead nurturing. By sending relevant and engaging content to leads at different stages of the sales funnel, businesses can keep prospects interested and informed, gradually moving them closer to making a purchase decision.

Driving Traffic to Websites and Landing Pages: Emails serve as a means to direct recipients to specific landing pages or sections of the company's website. This enables businesses to promote their latest blog posts, special offers, or new products, increasing website traffic and engagement.

Encouraging Customer Engagement: Effective marketing emails encourage recipients to interact with the brand. Whether it's through asking for feedback, participating in surveys, or sharing content on social media, these emails foster engagement and two-way communication between the business and its customers.

Announcing Promotions and Discounts: Businesses often use marketing emails to announce exclusive promotions, discounts, or limited-time offers. This creates a sense of urgency and incentivizes recipients to take immediate action, driving sales and conversions.

Upselling and Cross-selling: Marketing emails provide opportunities to upsell to existing customers or cross-sell related products or services. Businesses can tailor emails to recommend complementary items by analyzing customer behavior and preferences, ultimately increasing average order value.

Event and Webinar Promotion: When businesses host events, webinars, or workshops, marketing emails help promote and invite attendees. They can send reminders, event details, and post-event follow-ups to keep participants engaged.

Building Customer Loyalty: Regularly engaging with customers through marketing emails helps build loyalty and long-term relationships. Sending personalized offers, exclusive content, and appreciation emails makes customers feel valued and appreciated.

Measuring and Analyzing Performance: Marketing emails are measurable, allowing businesses to track open rates, click-through rates, conversions, and other metrics. These insights enable companies to refine their email strategies for better results over time.

Complying with Regulations: As a business email expert, you'll also know that marketing emails must comply with relevant regulations, such as the CAN-SPAM Act (in the US) and GDPR (in the EU). Ensuring compliance helps maintain the company's reputation and legal standing.

Templates

V1. Product Announcement Email (#099)

Introducing Our New [Product Name] - Get Ready to be Amazed!

Dear [Recipient's Name],

We are thrilled to announce the launch of our latest innovation - [Product Name]! This cutting-edge [product type] is designed to revolutionize the way you [benefit]. With its state-of-the-art features and unbeatable performance, [Product Name] is a game-changer in the industry.

We're offering an exclusive introductory discount of [Discount Percentage]% on all pre-orders to celebrate this milestone. Don't miss this opportunity to be among the first to experience the future of [product category].

Click the link below to explore [Product Name] and secure your early-bird discount today!

[CTA Button: Explore [Product Name] Now]

Thank you for being a valued customer and joining us on this exciting journey.

Best regards,

[Your Name]

[Your Title]

[Company Name]

[Contact Information]

V2. Limited-Time Offer Email (#100)

Last Chance to Save [Discount Percentage]% - Only [X] Days Left!

Dear [Recipient's Name],

Time is running out to take advantage of our exclusive limited-time offer! For just [X] more days, you can enjoy a special [Discount Percentage]% discount on our entire range of [products/services].

Whether you're looking for [benefit 1], [benefit 2], or [benefit 3], our products are designed to exceed your expectations. Don't miss out on this incredible opportunity to elevate your [industry/niche] experience.

Visit our website before [Offer End Date] to redeem your discount using the [Discount Code] code.

[CTA Button: Shop Now]

Hurry; stocks are limited, and this offer won't be extended!

Best regards,

[Your Name]

[Your Title]

[Company Name]

[Contact Information]

V3. New Feature Announcement Email (#101)

Exciting News: [New Feature] Now Available!

Dear [Recipient's Name],

We're thrilled to share some exciting news with you! Our team has been hard at work, and we're delighted to introduce our latest feature - [New Feature]. This powerful addition enhances [specific functionality or benefit] and elevates your experience with our product.

Some of the benefits of [New Feature] include:

- [Benefit 1]
- [Benefit 2]
- [Benefit 3]

Upgrade to the latest version now to access [New Feature] and enjoy a more seamless and efficient [product/service] experience.

[CTA Button: Upgrade Now]

If you have any questions or need assistance, our support team is always here to help.

Best regards,

[Your Name]

[Your Title]

[Company Name]

[Contact Information]

V4. Event Invitation Email (#102)

You're Invited: Join Us at [Event Name]

Dear [Recipient's Name],

We're thrilled to extend an exclusive invitation to you for our upcoming event - [Event Name]. This promises to be an unforgettable experience where you can connect with industry experts, learn about the latest trends, and network with like-minded professionals.

Event Details:

Date: [Event Date]

Time: [Event Time]

Venue: [Event Venue]

RSVP: [RSVP Link]

Our lineup of speakers includes [Speaker 1], [Speaker 2], and [Speaker 3], each sharing valuable insights and expertise on [event theme/topics]. You don't want to miss this opportunity to gain a competitive edge in your field.

Secure your spot today by clicking the RSVP link above. We look forward to seeing you there!

Best regards,

[Your Name]

[Your Title]

[Company Name]

[Contact Information]

V5. Abandoned Cart Reminder Email (#103)

Forgot Something? Complete Your Purchase Now!

Dear [Recipient's Name],

We noticed that you left [Product Name] in your shopping cart without completing your purchase. We understand how busy life can get, but we wouldn't want you to miss out on the opportunity to enjoy [benefits of the product].

As a special incentive, we're offering an additional [Discount Percentage]% off your order if you complete your purchase within the next [X] hours.

[CTA Button: Complete Purchase Now]

Don't let this amazing deal slip away - click the button above to return to your cart and secure your [Product Name] at a discounted price.

If you have any questions or need assistance, feel free to reach out to our support team.

Best regards,

[Your Name]

[Your Title]

[Company Name]

[Contact Information]

V6. *Customer Testimonial Email* (#104)

Discover What Our Customers Are Saying About Us!

Dear [Recipient's Name],

At [Company Name], we take pride in delivering exceptional products and services that meet and exceed our customers' expectations. But don't just take our word for it - hear what some of our delighted customers have to say:

"[Customer Testimonial 1]" - [Customer Name]

"[Customer Testimonial 2]" - [Customer Name]

"[Customer Testimonial 3]" - [Customer Name]

We are immensely grateful for our customers' trust and are committed to delivering the same outstanding experience to you.

Explore more testimonials and see why [Company Name] is the preferred choice for [product/service] in the [industry/niche].

[CTA Button: Read More Testimonials]

Thank you for being part of our journey.

Best regards,

[Your Name]

[Your Title]

[Company Name]

[Contact Information]

V7. Seasonal Sale Email (#105)

Seasonal Savings: [Discount Percentage]% Off All [Products/Services]

Dear [Recipient's Name],

As the [season] is upon us, we're thrilled to spread some seasonal cheer with a special offer just for you! Enjoy a generous [Discount Percentage]% discount on our entire range of [products/services] and make this [occasion] even more special.

Whether you're shopping for yourself or looking for the perfect gift, our [products/services] are designed to delight you.

[CTA Button: Shop Now]

Hurry, this offer is available for a limited time only. Make the most of these seasonal savings before they're gone!

Best regards,

[Your Name]

[Your Title]

[Company Name]

[Contact Information]

V8. Customer Appreciation Email (#106)

A Heartfelt Thank You for Being Part of Our Journey!

Dear [Recipient's Name],

As we celebrate another milestone at [Company Name], we want to take a moment to express our sincerest gratitude for your continued support and loyalty. Your trust in us has been instrumental in our growth and success.

We're offering you an exclusive [Discount Percentage]% discount on your next purchase with us to show our appreciation. It's a small token of our thanks for being an invaluable part of our journey.

[CTA Button: Shop Now]

Once again, thank you for choosing [Company Name]. We look forward to serving you and exceeding your expectations in the future.

Best regards,

[Your Name]

[Your Title]

[Company Name]

[Contact Information]

V9. Pre-Sale Announcement Emai (#107)

Sneak Peek: Get Ready for Our Upcoming Sale!

Dear [Recipient's Name],

We're excited to announce that our much-awaited sale is soon approaching! As a valued customer, we wanted to give you an exclusive sneak peek before we open it to the public.

Get ready to enjoy incredible savings on a wide range of [products/services]. There's something for everyone from [benefit 1] to [benefit 2].

Mark your calendar for the sale's opening day: [Sale Start Date]. Make sure you're among the first to grab the best deals!

[CTA Button: Add to Calendar]

Thank you for being a part of our loyal customer community. We can't wait to see you at the sale!

Best regards,

[Your Name]

[Your Title]

[Company Name]

[Contact Information]

ENHANCING YOUR EMAIL COMMUNICATION SKILLS

Improving clarity and impact through formatting in business emails is essential to ensuring that your message is effectively communicated and well-received by the recipient. Proper formatting enhances readability, highlights key information, and professionally presents your message. Here are some tips to improve clarity and impact through formatting:

Keep Paragraphs Short: Long paragraphs can be daunting to read, especially in email format. Break your content into short paragraphs to make it easier for the recipient to digest the information. Each paragraph should focus on a single point or idea.

Utilize Bullet Points and Lists: Bullet points and lists effectively present information in a scannable format. Use them to highlight key points, features, benefits, or action items. Bulleted lists help to organize information and make it visually appealing.

Use Bold and Italics Sparingly: Emphasize important words or phrases by using bold or italics sparingly. This draws attention to specific information and makes it stand out from the rest of the text. However, avoid overusing these formatting options, as it can make the email look cluttered.

Incorporate White Space: White space, also known as negative space, refers to the blank areas between paragraphs and sections of text. Adding sufficient white space improves readability and makes the email less overwhelming. It also allows the recipient's eyes to rest between blocks of text.

Include Headings and Subheadings: Use clear and descriptive headings and subheadings when your email contains multiple sections or topics. This helps the recipient quickly navigate the content and find the necessary information. Headings also break up large chunks of text, making the email more scannable.

Use Consistent Fonts and Sizes: Stick to a professional and easy-to-read font style and size throughout the email. Using too many different fonts can make the email appear unprofessional and distracting. Consistency in fonts and sizes enhances the overall appearance and readability.

Add Visual Elements: Incorporate images, charts, or graphs to complement your message and make the email visually appealing. Visual elements can convey information more effectively than text alone and help engage the recipient.

Align Text and Margins: Proper alignment of text and margins gives your email a polished look. Align the text to the left for easy reading, and ensure that margins are consistent on all sides.

Test on Different Devices: Before sending the email, test it on various devices (desktop, mobile, tablet) and email clients to ensure the formatting appears as intended. This step is crucial to ensure your message is well-received, regardless of the recipient's device.

By implementing these formatting techniques, you can significantly improve the clarity and impact of your business emails. Clear, well-organized, and visually appealing emails are more likely to be read, understood, and acted upon by the recipients.

Using Visuals and Attachments Effectively

Using visuals and attachments effectively in business emails can significantly enhance communication and engagement. Visuals and attachments can improve your message and not overwhelm or distract the recipient. Consider the relevance and necessity of using visuals and attachments in each email to create a professional and impactful communication experience.

Here's how you can do it from a business email perspective:

Visuals in the Email Body

- **Use Relevant Images**: Incorporate visuals, such as product images, infographics, or charts, that are directly related to the content of your email. High-quality and relevant visuals can grab the recipient's attention and convey your message more effectively.

- **Brand Consistency**: Ensure the visuals align with your brand's identity, including colors, fonts, and style. Consistency helps reinforce your brand image and makes your emails easily recognizable.

- **Avoid Overloading**: Use visuals strategically and sparingly. Too many images can clutter the email and distract from the core message. Focus on one or two key visuals to maintain clarity.

Attachments

- **Use Appropriate File Formats**: Attachments should be in formats commonly accepted by most email clients, such as PDFs, Word documents, or JPG images. Avoid uncommon or large file formats that may cause compatibility issues.

- **Zip Large Attachments**: For large files, consider compressing them into a zip folder to reduce the overall size. This ensures the email doesn't take too long to load for the recipient.
- **Mention Attachments Clearly**: You have attached specific files for the recipient's reference in the email body. Be explicit about the purpose of the attachments and how they relate to the email's content.
- **Offer Alternative Links**: Some email clients may have strict security settings that block or quarantine attachments. To ensure recipients can access the files, consider providing alternative links where they can download the attachments securely.

Using Visuals and Attachments Together

- **Supplement Information**: Visuals and attachments can complement the email text by providing additional information or detailed explanations. For example, you can include a product brochure or user guide as an attachment to support a product announcement email.
- **Showcase Data**: Visuals like graphs or charts can more effectively present complex data than lengthy paragraphs. Attach spreadsheets or detailed reports when necessary, but highlight key findings in the email body using visuals.
- **Encourage Action**: Visuals and attachments can encourage the recipient to take specific actions, such as clicking a CTA button or downloading a coupon. Use visuals strategically to guide recipients toward the desired action.

Mobile Responsiveness

- Ensure that both visuals and attachments are optimized for mobile devices. Many people check emails on their smartphones, and a visually appealing and easily accessible email is essential for a positive user experience.

- Keep file sizes small: Large attachments can lead to slow loading times on mobile devices. Optimize image sizes and provide links to download attachments instead of embedding them directly.

Accessibility Considerations

- **Provide alt text for images**: For visually impaired recipients, include alternative text (alt text) for images, describing the content and purpose of the visual.
- **Choose accessible file formats**: Ensure that attachments can be easily accessed by people with disabilities, such as using text-based formats in addition to or instead of image-based formats.

Handling Email Overload and Inbox Organization

Handling email overload and maintaining an organized inbox is crucial for efficient business communication. Below are some tips to help you manage email overload and keep your inbox organized:

Prioritize Emails: Start by prioritizing your emails based on urgency and importance. Focus on emails that require immediate attention, such as client inquiries, urgent requests, or time-sensitive tasks. Use labels or tags to categorize emails by priority.

Set Specific Times for Email Checking: Avoid constantly checking your email throughout the day, as it can be distracting. Instead, set specific times to check and respond to emails. This way, you can dedicate focused blocks of time to handle emails efficiently.

Unsubscribe from Unnecessary Lists: Regularly review and unsubscribe from newsletters and mailing lists that no longer add value to your work. This helps reduce unnecessary clutter in your inbox.

Use Folders and Labels: Create folders or labels to categorize emails by project, client, or topic. Organizing emails this way makes it easier to find specific messages when needed.

Adopt the Two-Minute Rule: If an email can be addressed in less than two minutes, handle it immediately. Reply, delegate, or take necessary action to clear such emails quickly.

Use Email Filters: Set up email filters to automatically sort incoming messages based on sender, subject, or keywords. This way, emails will be sorted into relevant folders without manual intervention.

Archive Old Emails: Once you've addressed an email without needing it for reference, archive it. Archiving keeps your inbox clutter-free while ensuring you can access the email if needed later.

Delegate Effectively: If an email requires someone else's expertise or attention, delegate the task with clear instructions. This ensures that tasks are appropriately distributed and completed promptly.

Use Email Templates: Create and use email templates for common responses or inquiries. This saves time and ensures consistent communication with clients and colleagues.

Leverage Email Search Function: Instead of scrolling through your entire inbox, use the search function to find specific emails quickly. Enter relevant keywords or the sender's name to locate the desired message.

Schedule Regular Inbox Cleanup: Dedicate weekly or monthly time to declutter and organize your inbox. Delete or archive emails that are no longer relevant, and address pending tasks to keep your inbox up-to-date.

Consider Third-Party Email Management Tools: Explore third-party email management tools that can help you automate tasks, sort emails, and prioritize messages based on your preferences.

Strategies for Effective Communication in a Remote Work Environment

Effective communication is essential for maintaining productivity, collaboration, and positive work culture in a remote work environment. Here are some strategies to enhance communication from a business email perspective:

Choose the Right Communication Channels: Select appropriate communication channels based on the nature of the message. For quick updates or urgent matters, use instant messaging or chat platforms. Opt for more detailed discussions or formal communication via email or video conferencing.

Be Clear and Concise: In business emails, clarity is crucial. Clearly state the purpose of the email in the subject line and get to the main point in the opening sentences. Use concise language to convey information effectively.

Use Professional Language and Tone: Maintain a professional tone in your emails, just as you would in face-to-face interactions. Avoid using informal language or abbreviations that may be confusing or unprofessional.

Set Expectations for Response Times: Establish guidelines for email response times. This ensures that team members know when to expect a reply and helps prevent delays in communication.

Leverage the Power of Formatting: Use bullet points, headings, and bold text to highlight important information and make emails more scannable. This is especially important for conveying complex or detailed information.

Practice Active Listening: When communicating via email, ensure you read messages carefully to fully understand the sender's intent. If uncertain about any points, seek clarification before responding.

Encourage Feedback: Create an open environment where team members feel comfortable providing feedback. Encourage the use of "reply all" for relevant discussions, fostering transparent and inclusive communication.

Schedule Regular Video Meetings: While email is an essential communication tool, video conferencing allows for face-to-face interactions, building stronger connections among remote team members.

Use Email Signatures: Utilize email signatures consistently to provide essential contact information and other pertinent details. Signatures make it easier for recipients to reach out to the appropriate person.

Avoid Overloading with Emails: Be mindful of the number of emails you send to colleagues, and use email communication judiciously. Consider consolidating related information into a single email rather than sending multiple separate messages.

Be Mindful of Time Zones: When working with remote team members across different time zones, respect their working hours. If sending emails during non-working hours, consider using delayed delivery features to avoid disrupting their personal time.

Address Conflict Professionally: If conflicts arise in email exchanges, deal with them constructively. Focus on the issue at hand, avoid personal attacks, and consider discussing sensitive matters privately through direct messages or one-on-one video calls.

Share Important Updates: Use emails to communicate essential updates, policy changes, and important company news. Ensure the subject line reflects the urgency and relevance of the information.

Include Visuals: Incorporate visual elements like charts, graphs, or images in your emails to convey data or illustrate concepts more effectively.

Acknowledge Receipt of Emails: Send a brief acknowledgment email when you receive critical messages to assure the sender that their communication has been received.

By implementing these strategies for effective communication in a remote work environment, you can foster stronger collaboration, build trust among team members, and ensure everyone stays connected and informed despite physical distances.

Maintaining Confidentiality and Privacy in Email Communication

Maintaining confidentiality and privacy in email communication is paramount in the business world. Emails often contain sensitive information, such as financial data, proprietary information, personal details, and confidential agreements. Ensuring the security of this data helps protect your business, your clients, and your reputation. Here are some essential practices to uphold confidentiality and privacy in your business email communication:

Use Secure Email Providers: Choose reputable and secure email service providers that use encryption protocols to safeguard your messages during transit and at rest. Look for providers that offer end-to-end encryption for enhanced security.

Implement Strong Passwords: Encourage all employees to use strong passwords for their email accounts. Passwords should be unique and long; include a combination of letters, numbers, and special characters. Regularly update passwords to further protect against unauthorized access.

Enable Two-Factor Authentication (2FA): Enable 2FA for all email accounts to add an extra layer of security. With 2FA, users need to provide a second authentication factor, such as a one-time code sent to their mobile device, to log in successfully.

Educate Employees: Conduct regular training sessions on email security and best practices for maintaining confidentiality. Employees should be aware of the risks associated with sharing sensitive information via email and understand the procedures to follow for secure communication.

Avoid Sending Sensitive Information: Discourage the inclusion of highly sensitive data in email communications whenever possible. If sharing confidential information is necessary, consider using secure file transfer methods or encrypted attachments.

Encrypt Attachments: If you need to send confidential documents or files via email, encrypt them before attaching them to the message. This adds an extra layer of protection to the content, even if the email service uses encryption for transmission.

Be Cautious with Links: Avoid clicking on suspicious links or downloading files from unknown sources. Phishing attacks are prevalent, and hackers may try to gain access to sensitive information through deceptive emails.

Limit Access to Sensitive Emails: Only provide access to confidential emails to those individuals who genuinely need it. Implement role-based access control to ensure that sensitive information is not available to all employees.

Clear Workstations: Encourage employees to log out of their email accounts or lock their workstations when they step away from their desks. This prevents unauthorized access in their absence.

Regularly Update Software: Keep email software and security tools up to date to protect against known vulnerabilities and security threats.

Secure Mobile Devices: If employees access email on mobile devices, ensure that these devices are secured with passcodes or biometrics. Enable remote wiping features to erase data from lost or stolen devices.

Establish a Confidentiality Policy: Develop a comprehensive confidentiality policy that outlines the organization's expectations and guidelines for handling sensitive information through email and other communication channels.

By implementing these practices and fostering a culture of email security and confidentiality, businesses can mitigate the risks associated with email communication and protect sensitive information. It's essential to stay vigilant and adapt security measures as new threats emerge to maintain the confidentiality and privacy of email communication.

CONCLUSION

Commonly Used Email Abbreviations and Acronyms

Email abbreviations have become more adaptable as the written word has developed to keep up with fast communications and busy schedules. While email acronyms help us save time, shorten messages, and communicate more effectively, keeping track of dozens of permutations of full stops, capital letters, and initialisms can be confusing and have the opposite effect. Hence, note that some of these abbreviations and acronyms may be informal or colloquial, so it's essential to consider the context and audience when using them in professional email communication.

Here are some commonly used email abbreviations and acronyms:

- FYI - For Your Information
- ASAP - As Soon As Possible
- EOD - End of Day
- EOM - End of Message
- ETA - Estimated Time of Arrival
- FAQ - Frequently Asked Questions
- BTW - By The Way
- FYA - For Your Action
- AFAIK - As Far As I Know

- IMHO - In My Humble Opinion
- LOL - Laugh Out Loud
- TTYL - Talk To You Later
- BRB - Be Right Back
- OMG - Oh My God
- NP - No Problem
- NRN - No Reply Necessary
- OOO - Out of Office
- RSVP - Répondez S'il Vous Plaît (Please respond)
- TIA - Thanks In Advance
- IIRC - If I Recall Correctly
- PFA - Please Find Attached
- IMO - In My Opinion
- FWIW - For What It's Worth
- ICYMI - In Case You Missed It
- N/A - Not Applicable
- WRT - With Respect To
- HTH - Hope This Helps
- ROFL - Rolling On the Floor Laughing
- RTFM - Read The "Friendly" Manual (less polite version)
- NSFW - Not Safe For Work
- TBH - To Be Honest
- IDK - I Don't Know
- IRL - In Real Life
- A/S/L - Age/Sex/Location
- SOL - Sh** Out of Luck (informal)
- NVM - Never Mind
- FOMO - Fear Of Missing Out
- TL;DR - Too Long; Didn't Read
- HBU - How About You?
- SMH - Shaking My Head

- AYFKM - Are You F***ing Kidding Me? (informal)
- IMEI - International Mobile Equipment Identity
- NSA - No Strings Attached
- OOTO - Out Of The Office
- TTYTT - To Tell You The Truth
- POV - Point Of View
- POV - Privately Owned Vehicle (context-dependent)
- ROTFLMAO - Rolling On The Floor Laughing My A** Off (informal)
- WYWH - Wish You Were Here
- YW - You're Welcome

Useful Tools and Resources for Business Email Writing

When it comes to business email writing, several tools and resources can help you compose effective and professional emails. Here are some useful tools and resources to enhance your business email writing skills:

Grammarly is a powerful writing assistant that checks your emails for grammar, spelling, and punctuation errors in real-time. It also provides suggestions for improving clarity and tone, helping you write with confidence.

Hemingway Editor: The Hemingway Editor app helps you simplify and clarify your writing. It highlights complex sentences, passive voice, and adverbs, making your emails more concise and easier to read.

Thesaurus.com: Enhance your vocabulary and avoid repetitive language with Thesaurus.com. It provides synonyms and antonyms, enabling you to find the right words to express your ideas.

CoSchedule Headline Analyzer: Craft compelling email subject lines that increase open rates with the CoSchedule Headline Analyzer. This tool evaluates your subject lines' emotional appeal, word balance, and length to optimize engagement.

HubSpot Email Signature Generator: Create professional and customized email signatures with the HubSpot Email Signature Generator. A well-designed signature adds a touch of professionalism to your emails.

Canva: Canva is a user-friendly graphic design platform that allows you to create visually appealing email templates or images to include in your emails. It offers a wide range of templates and design elements.

Unsplash and Pixabay: Access high-quality, royalty-free images to include in your emails, making them visually engaging and attractive to recipients.

Email on Acid: Test your emails for compatibility across various email clients and devices with Email on Acid. This tool helps you identify and fix rendering issues, ensuring a consistent user experience.

The Gregg Reference Manual: A comprehensive guide to business writing, grammar, and punctuation, The Gregg Reference Manual is an authoritative resource for improving your writing skills.

Business Email Templates: Online resources and platforms like Microsoft Office templates or Google Workspace templates offer a variety of pre-designed business email templates that you can customize to suit your specific needs.

Email Marketing Platforms: If you're sending marketing emails to a large audience, consider using email marketing platforms like Mailchimp, Constant Contact, or SendinBlue. These platforms offer features for email design, list management, and tracking email campaign performance.

Business Writing Courses: Consider enrolling in online business writing courses or workshops offered by platforms like LinkedIn Learning, Udemy, or Coursera. These courses provide in-depth guidance on crafting effective business emails.

Business Email Writing Blogs and Guides: Explore blogs and guides dedicated to business email writing, such as HubSpot's blog or the Business Writing section on The Balance Careers. These resources offer valuable tips and insights.

While tools and resources can be beneficial, continuous practice and refinement of your business email writing skills are essential for long-term improvement. Tailor your emails to the specific needs of your audience, maintain professionalism, and strive for clarity and conciseness in your communication.

Summary

In conclusion, "Business Email Writing: 99+ Essential Message Templates for Unstoppable Communication Skills at Work" is a comprehensive guide that equips you with the knowledge and tools to excel in email communication within a professional setting. You have seen that the book focuses on developing effective business email writing skills by providing essential message templates for a wide range of scenarios.

Throughout the book, readers learn the importance of clear and concise communication, tailoring emails to different audiences, and avoiding common mistakes that can hinder effective communication. They gain insights into the essential components of a business email, including subject lines, greetings, body content, closing remarks, and signatures.

The book offers a wealth of email templates for various situations, including networking emails, professional correspondence, sales and marketing emails, customer service emails, internal communication, and job application and interview emails. These templates serve as practical examples to guide readers in crafting impactful messages that achieve their intended objectives.

Furthermore, the book delves into writing techniques, such as maintaining a professional tone, using proper grammar and punctuation, and enhancing email clarity and readability. It emphasizes the importance of proofreading and editing to present polished and error-free emails.

By following the book's guidance and leveraging its templates and resources, readers can enhance their communication skills, build stronger professional relationships, and achieve success in their respective fields. "Business Email Writing: 99+ Essential Message Templates for Unstoppable Communication Skills at Work" serves as an indispensable tool for anyone seeking to master the art of effective business email communication, making it an invaluable addition to any professional's toolkit.

www.ingramcontent.com/pod-product-compliance
Lightning Source LLC
Chambersburg PA
CBHW071606210326
41597CB00019B/3420